MW01709475

The Last 10 Years

Matthew J Dean

The Last 10 Years

tellwell

Tellwell Talent
www.tellwell.ca

ISBN
978-0-2288-2037-6 (Hardcover)
978-0-2288-2035-2 (Paperback)
978-0-2288-2036-9 (eBook)

Special thanks to all those who helped finish off Matt's book.

Listing all the names

Alyssa Dean

Gemma Dean

Andrew Dean

Joshua Dean

Betty Dean

Greg Callan

Amy Long

Andrea Barry

Mattheu and Anny Gognon

Amber Smith-Comé

Gavin and Clare Fuller

Table of Contents

The Beginning

As I sit here in the hospital with my beautiful wife and our adorable newborn, I am overwhelmed with joy but at the same time immense sorrow because I know my life is ending. My body grows weaker with every breath. I will not see my children grow up and what they will become. I will not get to care for them when they call out my name or when they need me. I will never be able to help them as I await my rapidly approaching and inevitable death. I should be the happiest man on the planet, but I can't stop thinking about ending my life.

My name is Matt Dean and I have ALS. I was recently diagnosed with ALS and it sucks. It sucks period. One of the suckiest diseases going. As bad as it sounds, when they were trying to figure out what was wrong with me, they told me that it could be a brain tumor — I was hoping it was a tumor because there was a chance at recovery. ALS is unyielding and relentless, with a 100% kill rate. It kills you slowly so you get a front row seat to watch yourself die a little bit each day. ALS is not like other diseases. I won't get better. It is not currently possible. With most diseases there is hope for a cure and for getting better. I can only hope that the new drug will be able to slow it down so I get more time with my family.

I was never in tip-top shape or peak physical fitness (do my teens count when I could eat anything and do anything and still have a sort of six pack? Probably not), but I was always good at sports and very co-ordinated. At the stage I am at now I struggle to dress myself and wipe my own bum. Do you understand how demoralising that is? I used to be able to make it rain hookshot threes on the basketball court, do spinaramas on the ice to elude a defender, run the bases at Major League speed, throw anything at anything and hit it, and basically anything else I wanted. Now I can barely tie my shoes. I fall over regularly because my balance is so out of whack. It is as if I am on a rowboat in the middle of the sea during hurricane season.

How am I to weather this storm? How am I to trudge on when I can no longer control whether I laugh or cry? I am not capable any longer. I rely on all of my family and friends to help. Isn't that too much to ask? I don't want help but I know that without it, I can't always get out of bed or pull my T-shirt over my moobs. T-shirts actually get stuck on my moobs and I no longer have the dexterity to manoeuvre my hand to the right place to pull them down.

I am writing this book on my smartphone because I can no longer type but my thumbs still work quite well. So where should I start this tale? The beginning, the middle or the end? Some would argue that I should start at the beginning but the best part of my life really has been the last 10 years. I will throw in some great little stories from my past here and there where pertinent.

Quick update: I'm typing the rest of this book with my eyes now as I have pretty much lost the use of my hands.

My timeline with the disease

September 2017

Twitching began in my left bicep

October 2017

Twitching still in my left bicep

Broke my tailbone falling after a routine move during a hockey game

November 2017

The twitching began in my right bicep and continued in my left bicep

Sought medical advice and testing began on my nerves

Co-ordination began to be affected while doing complex athletic movement, which I attributed to aging

December 2017

Twitching began to spread to other parts of my body

First week-long hospital admission for testing

At times struggled with fine motor skills, and I fell playing floorball for no reason

January 2018

Could no longer run and fell during a game of floorball a couple of times

Second hospital admission for a week of testing

Writing on the chalkboard becomes more challenging

Start to notice that my grip is weakening

February 2018

Tying shoes becomes more challenging
Voice started changing
I started to become more emotional and I could not control it
Diagnosed with **ALS!**

March 2018

Started to have noticeable weaknesses and lack of coordination!
Play basketball for the last time struggling to dribble and
I can't throw the ball high enough to make a basket
Play floorball for the last time falling over a
few times and not being able to do
anything co-ordinated
Change in my voice is more pronounced

April 2018

Could no longer walk normally
Started having challenges with my speech and swallowing!
Could no longer sing properly at all
Struggle with personal care and going to the bathroom
Could no longer shave my head
Stairs become difficult without the use of the railing
Typing becomes harder
All fine motor skills are weakening

May 2018

Walking for a long distance is no longer possible without help
Getting in and out of vehicles requires assistance if there is no handle
Tying of shoes is increasingly a challenge
Feeding myself is starting to become harder
Showering is starting to become a challenge
Dressing myself independently is tricky, and
I sometimes require assistance
Voice is more drunk-like and I am starting to struggle with words
My voice is starting to no longer sound like mine
Breathing at night requires a BiPAP machine

June 2018

Walking becomes more difficult and I started using a wheelchair
This is the last month that I feed, bathe and dress myself
I had a poop accident in Banff and my sister had
to help me while I cried. Not many accessible
bathrooms in Banff so we went to the hospital
This is the last month that I tie my own shoes
Coughing becomes almost impossible
Breathing is weakening
Minor cramping in my back and legs

July 2018

Gemma now dresses, feeds, showers and
wipes me…I do mean my bum
No more tying my shoes
I need Gemma to shadow me by the stairs only
Voice and breathing continue to decline
Minor cramping in my back and legs

August 2018

This is the last month that I walk a short distance unaided
My hands are almost closed from the disease
Voice continues to get worse and more slurring occurs
Minor cramping in my back and legs

September 2018

Gemma now walks with me everywhere for
support and helps with all toileting
Voice is worse and people are starting to have
trouble understanding some words
Hands are closed but are easily opened without pain
Minor cramping in my back and legs
Arms lose almost 50% rotation

October 2018

Transfer belt is introduced and it is permanent
Balance is getting worse, and I need something
or someone to hold on to
People are starting to ask me to repeat myself
Hands experience pain when opened
Major cramping and spasms occur in my back and legs

November 2018

Transfer belt and wheel chair used
I can no longer sleep in the hospital bed so
move to recliner during the night
I use a urinal to go to the toilet
Cramping continues in back, legs and shoulders

December 2018

Speech is really bad and most people don't understand
me. Gemma helps to decipher what I am saying
Hospital bed removed and a recliner is put into the bedroom
Cramping all the time
Hands are painful
Swallowing certain foods has become increasingly difficult

January 2019

It all sucks!

Chapter One

How I Got Into Teaching

Where do I begin? I started working for the Tim Horton Children's Ranch in the summer of 1998 and finished at winter camp in 2001. I returned this year for the first time in three and a half years. I was camping in the area with other camp alumni, some of whom I had not seen since I had left. Yet it seemed like we had never missed a beat. I was so excited — actually nervous — about visiting the camp. I was not sure how I would feel returning to Kananaskis. The environment we shared at the Tim Horton Children's Foundation allowed us to forge friendships that will stand the test of time. And it got me thinking: if camp was so positive for me what was it like for the campers?

By then we were pulling into camp, my thoughts were put on hold. It was like I had never left. You see, this place holds a special place in my heart. It had taken a hold of me from the moment I first arrived. Its beauty is raw and powerful, and now even more so. It was here I decided I would become a teacher. It was because of the children who attended the camp that I chose this path. Each passing session was unique and had their moments, but the smiles made all of the difference. It was the sharing of camp experiences between staff and camper that makes this place so wonderful. For the gift that those children gave me, I will forever be thankful. I only wish what I did for them would measure up to what they did for me.

Summer Adventure: Finding a Job

It all started one gloomy day when I was slogging through the muddy trenches of yet another labourer's typical quest: the completion of the perfect ditch. You see, I was working for Harwood's Plumbing and Heating as a general labourer, digging trenches and installing toilets. I had the day off and I went up to the college with Elliott. I was passing the job board for summer employment when this peculiar black symbol caught my eye. As I approached the elderly piece of off-white paper that must have once shone brightly like a fresh photocopy, my curiosity began to heighten. I quickly read the piece of paper, lapping up the information like a black dog sipping from his dish on a hot summer's day. I jotted down the address and phone number, slipped it in my back pocket and headed towards Elliott's class where I promised I would meet him. Later that same afternoon Elliott and I proceeded to the Youth Employment Centre to look for summer jobs. We glanced over the job postings and they were of the typical sort in North Bay: scarce and low paying. While I was there, I played my hunch and faxed my resume to the number on the intricately folded paper once removed from my ass pocket. Five minutes later, Elliott and I headed home to Callander for what was the beginning of my summer.

Summer Adventure: The Phone Call

I remember like it was yesterday. I had just returned from my weekend visiting family in St. Catharines (June 1, 2). My mom and I had an interesting discussion on the way home about my plans for the summer. I told her I hadn't found anything yet and was still looking for employment. I had intentions of moving back to St. Catharines and working at the Canadian Tire full-time. The drive home was nothing unusual, not a lot of traffic and the same probing questions from my mother.

"Are you going to go to school in the fall?"
"How are you going to earn tuition money?"

I thought I had an answer to these questions in St. Catharines, but when I stepped out of the car and walked the short walk to my house, little did I know my life was about to change forever. I opened the door where I was greeted by my overly hyperactive dog. He almost knocked me over. Out of habit I asked if anyone had called for me. Andrew, my younger brother (I no longer refer to him as my little brother because he stands 6'4" and he is only 15), said Tim Horton's called for me. I was puzzled and didn't understand right away. I went to the calendar because I know some people who work at Timmy's in North Bay. I looked at the number written neatly along the bottom of the calendar and to my surprise it was an Alberta area code. Then I remembered the faded piece of paper with a black logo. I couldn't believe it, I was astonished, awestruck — call it what you will, but I could hardly contain my excitement. I called the number immediately without a single hesitation. I dialled the number in record time. The tension mounted with every ring. Then there was a pause; the brief silence seemed to last forever.

"Tim Horton's Children's Ranch, Jason speaking."

"Hello, my name is Matthew J. Dean. It is to my understanding you called for me a couple of days ago."

"Yes, as a matter of fact I did. What are you doing for summer employment?"

"Nothing right now, but I have a job offer in St. Catharines for full-time work."

"Would you be interested in working here for the summer?"

Without even thinking I said, "YES."

"I am very busy right now but I will call you later for an interview."

"I will be right here," I replied with some enthusiasm — you know, to make him believe I was really excited, although I am sure he could tell already.

"Thank you for returning my call and I will call you in the next couple of days to conduct an interview," he said.

"Thank you for your consideration, Sir."

That was that and I waited patiently for the interview

Matt's Summer Adventure: The Interview

A couple of days went by and I had heard nothing. I felt like he forgot about me, and that he wasn't even going to call me back.

That's when I said enough is enough, picked up the portable phone from the charger and dialled the number. The prolonged ringing gave me another empty feeling of despair. For a brief moment I thought about hanging up, calling my aunt in St. Catharines and taking the job at the Canadian Tire. As I refocused my energy to paying attention to the ringing noise coming out of the phone, somebody answered.

"Hello, Tim Horton's Children's Ranch, Jason speaking."

"Hi, this is Matt Dean calling."

"Oh, geez I forgot to call you, didn't I?"

"I was just wondering where I stood in your employment plans."

"Are you available at around 4:00 p.m. my time for an interview?"

"That is no problem, I was planning on sitting down to read the Bible and practice my preaching." OK, that's a bogus line. This is what I really said:

"I would be glad to."

"Alright then I will call you at four."

"Great I'll talk to you later, goodbye."

"Bye."

This all took place at about 5:30 p.m. on the 4th of June, so the interview was not that far away. The minutes drifted by very slowly and every premature telephone ring before six was nothing but a pain in the fart-o-matic. I grew impatient and had to pee to relieve some of the tension. As I put the seat down and flushed it was almost six o'clock. I twiddled my thumbs as I hummed the Tim Horton's jingle (Hmmmm hmmmm hmmmm hmmmm hmmmm Tim Horton's). Just then the phone rang. Instinctively I let out a Braveheart-like war cry:

"I GOT IT!" I then picked up the phone.

"Hello, could I speak to Matt Dean please."

"Speaking."

"This is Jason Evanson from the Tim Horton's Children's Ranch in Kananaskis, Alberta. How are you this afternoon?" He sounded pretty nervous, almost as nervous as me.

"Great, how are you? Pretty busy?" I figured I'd get to know him a little before he started the interview. It's never too early to start kissing ass. He then proceeded with a long list of questions and anecdotes in a big long blur that lasted about twenty minutes to half an hour. I can hardly remember most of the questions, probably because I lied through the skin of my teeth. Then came the final question:

"Would you be interested in working here for the summer?"

"Yes, yes I would," (apply voiceover from lunch lady Doris of *The Simpsons*). I was so excited and luckily for me I peed earlier or I would have been a little wet.

"Can you make it here by June 9 for staff training?"

Without even thinking about it I let out a huge "YES, no problem!"

"You will need a criminal check done and the rest of your background information."

"No problem. I'll see you on the ninth."

"Great, welcome aboard."

With all of that said and done I hung up the phone, ran down the stairs and told my parents the good news. I packed up the belongings I'd need based on the list Jason faxed to Elliott's place. As I prepared my luggage, my dog gave me the worst look I had ever seen (from a dog). My family was fine with me leaving again, but Hershey on the other hand seemed a little miffed.

I was on the road again. Well, almost. I took care of all the necessary business on the fifth and boarded the bus on the sixth around two or three in the morning. I couldn't get a plane ticket on such a short notice, and if I did it would have cost me an arm and a leg. My loving mother bought me a round trip bus ticket that would last forty-nine hours there and forty-nine hours back.

Summer Adventure: The Bus Ride

I woke up bright and early on the sixth of June. My loving mother woke me up from my dormant state. I was dreaming of all the cool things I was going to do this summer and the new people. I had a shower to wake myself up and a bowl of porridge to fill the hunger gap. My mom told me to hurry so I wouldn't miss the bus. We loaded my baggage into the car and I returned inside to take one last pee and to give my dog a kiss goodbye. I couldn't find Hershey right away, he was a little pissed that I decided to leave again and not bring him with me. I said I wouldn't be gone that long and that I would miss him. I gave him a hug and a kiss goodbye and closed the door behind me. My mom and I didn't speak very much on the way to the bus station that morning but that was to be expected because I was finally going to do something with my life — for the summer anyways. I arrived at the bus station with about fifteen minutes to spare and bought a round trip ticket and then boarded the bus.

Well the bus ride started out just as any other long potential case of hemorrhoids. My first stop was Sudbury (Yawn — been there done that, livin' it) for a few minutes then on to Sault Ste. Marie. When I was in the Sault I decided to go for a walk to the closest mall and by some food for the long trip. As I was walking through the mall I realised what I was about to do. I was cruising through an unknown mall by myself. I wish I would have done that ride with someone, boy did it suck. Anyway, I returned to the bus station and boarded the bus again. This time the next main stop was Thunder Bay. I was looking forward to it because I have a friend there. Well, actually she lives in Murillo. So I was on my way again pulling out of the Greyhound station in the Sault and onwards towards the unknown.

Well there isn't too much in Northern Ontario if you've been there before. Some people here and there and a hell of a lot of lakes and trees. I stopped in some little towns on the way, like Marathon and White River (and I thought my town was small). I was almost by myself the whole time on the bus, there weren't too many people. There might have been ten people all the way to Thunder Bay. So what could I say, except I was pretty tired and hit the hay. This all happened in the same day, no way. It's true I say.

Anyway, the ride wasn't that exciting, and as we got closer to Thunder Bay I think I saw three cars on the highway (all beer trucks). Finally around ten o'clock we pulled into Thunder Bay (I am just going to abbreviate the damn city from now on). I went to the phone and called my friend, Ydnew. She wasn't home. *Great*, I thought, *the only person I knew within 1000 km and she's not home.* I decided I would just try Ydnew again to see if she really wasn't home for sure.

For instance, she could have been indisposed at the moment I had made my previous phone call. Ring, ring, ring (if you didn't know, that is the sound the telephone makes when it's ringing). I didn't think I was going to get an answer but on the fourth ring someone picked up.

"Hello?" he said in a husky voice.

"Hi there, could I speak to Ydnew Ynneh (changing names because of the provision in the Privacy Act, section 2.a-paragraph C) PLEASE," I replied, a little over zealous.

"Yeah sure, she just came in."

The tension on the cable was pretty thick.

"Hi, this is Ydnew."

"Is this the Ydnew Ynneh that was on Katimavik?"

"Yes, may I ask who is calling?"

"Wendy it's me and I'm in TB."

"Ttam, oh my god! Where exactly are you? I'm coming."

"The bus station."

"Great, I'll be there soon."

"I'm only going to be here for an hour."

"That's OK"

"Great. See you soon."

Within the next twenty-five minutes my friend Ydnew pulled up in her white car. Then we proceeded to rehash old times in the lovely bus station cafeteria. Sorry, what took place in the conversation probably wouldn't interest you so I'll leave it out. An hour later I boarded the bus for Winnipeg. As I got on the bus I waived a fond farewell to my Katima-buddy and sat down by this really cute girl. I turned to the window to see my friend waving at me, so I returned the wave with a little emotion in it, just to show I was going to miss her. As the bus pulled out of the parking lot I saw my friend's little white car driving off into the darkness with its tail-lights ever growing dimmer. *Man does my ass hurt*, I thought. I tried to sleep on the bus but I just couldn't. Not only did this make me feel terrible, but I was so disoriented I didn't know what day it was or how long I had been riding. We stopped at the Robin's Donuts in Kenora, and I was so happy to stretch my legs and back and let my ass breathe. We re-boarded the bus about twenty minutes later and headed west towards Winnipeg. We stopped in Dryden or something like that for a smoke break then pressed on.

We arrived at Winnipeg just after sunrise and we were going to be there for more than an hour, so I decided to call my friend Eilsel in Brandon and see if she would like to visit. She said she had to work but she would lie (only a white lie so it was OK) and come and pick me up at the bus station when I got there and take me for a tour of Brandon (home of the Wheat Kings). After I hung up the phone I decided to take a walk. I walked out of the station and to my surprise there was nothing moving — no cars, no people, no anything. I walked down the street towards the infamous parliament building. It was so beautiful that morning I decided to sit down on the steps and have a nice ice cold glass of Gatorade that I had previously prepared in the bathroom of the bus station (Hey, you don't have to keep tabs on me all the time). I hung out there for about 15-20 minutes and then made my way back to the bus station to catch the westbound bus again. I wish I could have stayed longer in Winnipeg but I had to follow my destiny.

When I got to Brandon, my friend Eilsel met me. She took me to her house where she took my hand and showed me to her room where we engaged in a stimulating conversation about old Katima-stuff. After that I went for a quick ride around Brandon in Eilsel's car; the town looks pretty cool. Hey — I just drove around, I never got the chance to explore. The hour flew by like Hurricane George on a Sunday. I was back on the bus before I knew it and off to Regina.

When I left Brandon I had no idea the prairies were actually like that. This is where I also got my first real bit of sleep. However, that was until somewhere in the middle of Saskatchewan that I was woken up by a one-eyed French nun asking, "ou est la salle de bain?" This startled me only a little... Who am I kidding? I thought that the bus had perished in some fiery crash. Then I remembered where I was and knew that was highly unlikely. I mean I had heard stories, but man oh man was I ever surprised. Perhaps I had better explain. Many years ago I learned from a wise man that the Great Prairies used to be a large inland sea that spawned a diverse array of species. Perhaps I shall explain this a little further. From this miracle sea that disappeared after the glaciers retreated post the last ice age, all of the marine life that used to be was now largely buried deep beneath the fertile soils (another main reason the soils are fertile is because of the decaying animal matter and stuff) and converted through geological processes to produce things that we hold dear to our lives, different forms of ENERGY.

What was I talking about? Oh yeah, the prairies are flatter than a dead skunk on the Trans Canada baby. So as I rolled into Regina this guy I met on the bus from Sudbury (oh, what a coincidence) asked me if I knew where to go in Regina to eat. I said no, so we decided that there had to be a Subway close to the bus station. As we aimlessly walked around downtown, we figured we had better get directions from some of the nice young people. The directions they gave us were the poops and by the time we found Subway it was closed. So we had to settle for some Chinese at Mama something or other.

I got back on the bus just in time to leave for Calgary. We rolled into Calgary on the morning of June 8. I asked my friend, Nerrad, to pick me up at the bus station. He arrived shortly after I got there and we went back to his place. Man, are Katima-buddies great or what? That night we drank some beer — as in root — and went to a couple of bars — as in "nightclubs." Hehehe, no one knows we went to the nudie (oops better delete that. Phew that was close). Anyway, after hanging out in Calgary we went back to his place where he asked me to taste some of the new Nestle products that had just came out. Man oh man were they good. We then drank beer and played guitar.

I never thought I'd say this, but man I was pretty nervous about what was to take place the next day: PRE-CAMP...

Matt's Summer Adventure: PRE-CAMP

I hope everything is going well and everyone is still having some fun.

Well, to begin I had better begin from the beginning of that day on June 9. I awoke from my slumber at around 10:30 in the morning in the basement of my friend's house where I had slept on very a comfortable couch. Why are other people's couches so damn comfortable — can anyone answer that? Anyways, my friend Nerrad asked me what time I would like to leave for camp.

"I don't have to be there until one, so how long will it take us to get there?" I said.

"Probably an hour or so."

"Well, how about we leave at 11:30?"

"OK, so that's when we'll leave," he said with a disappointed tone vibrating off his palate.

We ate our breakfast of bagels and smarties ice cream, packed my things and loaded the truck. We had a relatively long ride ahead of us so we stocked up on beer and nachos. As we pulled out of the driveway we cracked open a couple of Buds and Nerrad turned to me and handed me his CD cases and said "You DJ, I trust you." With my ice cold suds in one hand and a whole stack of CDs in the other, I thought, *What a great way to start the day.* As I flipped through his CDs I pulled out some Tragically Hip. I chugged the rest of my beer and tossed the can out the window. Man did that sucker ever bounce — it was very graceful bouncing on the asphalt almost like the can itself was a delicate ballerina dancing in the wind. Just kidding! Like my friend and I would drink and drive. The only thing that we drank in that truck was beer, as in root.

We had no problems finding the camp because the directions were straightforward and simple. As we pulled up to the camp, we were in awe. I mean I had never been to a summer camp before, let alone worked at one. I thought it looked pretty posh. We parked alongside the big vans and it reminded my friend and I of Katimavik. I didn't take my gear out of the back of the truck because I wasn't sure if this was for real yet or not. I didn't know were to go when I noticed one of the double doors at the side of the lodge swung open. Out walked this fragile young man with gargantuan rings of pit sweat around his underarms. I thought my friend was going to start laughing.

"Hi! I'm the camp director, Jason Evanson."

"Hi my name is Ttam Naed and this is my friend Nerrad."

"Pleased to meet you, so how was your trip? Weren't you the one that took the bus all the way here from Ontario?"

"Pleased to meet you as well, never again will I ever ride the bus for that long. Never again."

"We can go on a little tour and then you can take your stuff to cabin 6."

"Great."

Ah cabin six, the cabin where it all began. We proceeded to the lodge and Jason showed us around in the lodge upstairs and downstairs. Upstairs was wicked, there was a bar, pool table, TV and VCR, stereo, fireplace, couches and chairs, oh my. Downstairs had everything the upstairs did but the TV was bigger (satellite TV), so was the stereo. I couldn't help but feel really good about my new job. We then headed down the path towards cabin 6 and down the hill towards flag circle and the rec centre. The rec centre was pretty impressive in its own right; it was fairly large and that meant floor hockey would be fun. The little tour was great, and we finished up at the lodge by the pond. He said he would have to go and do some work and I could take my stuff to cabin 6.

Ah cabin six, the cabin where it all began. My friend Nerrad helped me carry all of my belongings to cabin 6. Ah cabin six, the cabin where it all began. I was the first one there, I know this because when I opened the door there was no one else in the cabin. I made my way to the bunk beds and selected the bottom bunk mainly because when I was on Katimavik my roommate (Ueihtam) always took the top bunk and I took the bottom bunk. I snooped around the cabin and to my delight there was a welcome bag full of treats. There was a toothbrush, candy so you could make use of the toothbrush, some OJ, fabric softener, a cup commemorating the grand opening of the camp on June 22 (which happens to be my birthday: hint hint, wink wink, nudge nudge) in 1991, and some other things I don't recollect. I unpacked some of my things and then walked with my friend back to his truck and we said goodbye. Actually it was more along the lines of "I'll see you later Big Nuts."

As I watched my friend drive away I began to realise I was alone now and there doesn't seem to be anyone around, I think I'm alone now and there doesn't seem to be anyone around. Tiffany, wasn't she great? (I'm talking about the entertainer — man was she hot or what when we were little kids?) Anyway my point is I was alone, I didn't know anybody and I was a little nervous, weren't you? I went to the lodge where the first person I met was, uh, let's call him Bor. He introduced himself and we began chatting. He told me that he worked for Timmy's last year and had a lot of fun. Before Timmy's he worked in the field (really he did) working with seismic equipment. He also played guitar.

The rest of the day was basically used to get acquainted with everybody. We had pizza and juice or pop to satisfy the hunger. I was still pretty nervous because I was a rookie. I had overheard other counsellors speaking about where they had worked and I was feeling a little intimidated. Actually I really felt out of place. I didn't know if I was going to fit in. Then I saw a couple of guys, the two Bors, acting a little...let's just say crazy...and then I knew I was going to fit in, but first I had to adjust.

Making the adjustment was easy, the people were great and very open. Later that day I met the boys from cabin 6. Ah cabin six, the cabin where it all began. Let's see there was Sivad, Kram and last but definitely not least Sivraj. The friendships and bonds that were made with these guys were instantaneous. We all got along very well and had a great time together. The first night is a very sketchy one in my memory at the current moment, but I am sure you remember what we did. I watched a little TV that night with some of the guys. I was pleased to find out that Sivad also played the guitar and he was extremely good, but of course I'm sure you already knew that (Ace Ventura thing again).

I am glad I brought my alarm clock because we had to get up pretty early the next morning for flag circle. I really liked flag circle — what a great way to wake up in the morning. We sang our national anthem and then heard a quote of the day and headed up Cardiac Hill for breakfast. The reason it is called Cardiac Hill is because it is a pain the cardiac to walk up. Breakfast was good. The kitchen staff was excellent. Oh man, I never ate that well before (I'm talking about at a job — sorry, no one can top my mom or my Nonie). The rest of the day was get acquainted and play camp games. Most importantly we started singing songs, songs I had never heard before. It was all a little strange but it was still a lot of fun. Over the next couple of days, cabin 6 became very close and we invented a song for when you felt a little uptight in a certain area. It is called the *Pooh-pooh Song*. For those who were fortunate enough to hear it, remember it is still being played and will never die.

Summer Adventure: The Jarvina Scandal

Well, to begin I would just like to say there are a lot of myths circulating about the origin of Jarvina. Perhaps I had better begin with the starting of camp as I became friends with the boys of cabin six. Ah cabin six, the cabin where it all began. We played basketball a lot during pre-camp. This is where I made my friends the quickest. I really enjoyed our pre-camp basketball games. The court was graced regularly by camp legends. This was also my first encounter with Yrrek. I thought it was odd that this girl watched us for a while, so I decided to ask her if she wanted to play. Do you know what she said? "I might get sweaty." I mean really — what was she thinking?

"Well you can shoot with us for a while and if you feel like playing you are more than welcome."

"OK, maybe I'll shoot with you guys for bit."

She really drew that out just to make us think she really didn't know what she was doing. She shot alright and made us all look like slack-jawed nimble-footed bball wannabes and hardly broke a sweat. Then came what I had already predetermined: she became a little sweaty and had to remove the shirt. Sweat-shirt that is. I gazed at her T-shirt and read the bold lettering "DINO'S BASKETBALL." Might get sweaty my ass. She was just worried about deflating our egos and mixing estrogen with testosterone and ultimately embarrassing the boy counsellors to the point where she would not be welcome. This must have been what she was pondering because she would have jumped right in if she felt welcome. Don't you think?

Well, after she took us to school and then some she felt a little more at ease. At Least that is what I had duly noted from my observations. But what she didn't take into consideration was she was playing with some nice guys who didn't place; perhaps place isn't the right word — more like "set limits" on her because she was a girl. We all stank and had no problem letting a girl dominate what was rightfully hers. I mean really guys, there comes a time when we have to admit to ourselves that it is OK to let a girl dominate you, I mean over you. Yeah that's it, over you. So anyway, we had a really good workout and were a little stinky and smelly and sweaty. We decided to return to the cabin (cabin six that is — Ah cabin six, the cabin where it all began). We figured we'd take turns in the shower by who ever was ready first. I was standing by my bunk when I heard something from Sivraj's room.

"Hey guys, have you ever seen my sister? Her name is Jarvina."

"What the hell are you talking about" I hollered. I hollered because my little .001 watt tape recorder was just a booming. I believe that the tune playing at the time was *Stayin Alive* by Wyclef.

"Fellas, meet my sister Jarivna." On his face was the dirtiest grin only Sivraj could make.

"Oh my god that is the grossest thing I have ever seen!" declared Sivad, with a slight smile.

"AAAAAAAHHHHHHHHHHHHHH" shouted Kram in disgust while trying to hide his shrewd, bearded snicker.

"That is the ugliest looking sister I have ever seen," I said trying to hold in the laughter. But sooner or later if you bottle something up inside it will come out with a vengeance, and mine came out almost immediately. We all started laughing our heads off. It was the funniest pre-camp moment because it provided good solid laughter all summer long, especially during the talent show. I'm sure everyone remembers the talent show. Sivad and I danced like *The Full Monty*, which is where I eventually received my nickname (for the girls and Sivraj, you know where it really came from). The two wild and crazy girls who were trying to brush each other's teeth (later to be named Darte and Wookie). *The Red Green Show* with the weird new guy who seemed a little out of place (later coined the phrase "DOOOOOIT"). Then three guys who could not control their laughter at all during their skit of a band of drummers playing a song that sounds like what I am about to write:

"ting, Jarvina, WAAH - ting, Jarvina, WAAH."

It was so funny, so now I am sure since you now know where Jarvina came from you will find this much more interesting and perhaps even more funny. Stay tuned for the next chapter in Matt's summer adventure:

Summer Adventure: The Staff Overnight and Salt Bet

Sorry this is a little later than I had hoped. I was on a good pace there for a while but I'm not too sure now if the book will be done before my school year is. Anyway, on with the story.

As pre-camp approached its end, the staff grew closer together and were excited about the staff overnight. You see, the staff overnight determined a lot of things for me and I'm sure a couple of you too. I was really anticipating the staff overnight because I was going to put the moves on Blush (whenever she gets embarrassed her face immediately turns a bright red). I have decided to skip the day where we all received our nicknames because it happened after the staff overnight. So from now on I will try to accurately describe in parenthesis a phrase or sentence about their name.

Since there were not enough horses for all of the staff to ride, a few volunteers decided to make the walk. I was impressed with my horse, Midnight, because she is the biggest sweetheart in the entire world. On the way up I had some interesting conversations with a few of the counsellors but most importantly my horse. You see, I have a tendency of being able to communicate with animals sort of like Dr. Doolittle, and Midnight could sense that so we discussed some of the moral issues that plague today's society. Anyway I don't want to bore you with that conversation so we'll just move ahead to the overnight sight.

As everyone arrived and de-horsed I was kind of excited because this was going to be a special night. This was the end part of my master plan. This was where I was going make my first move and seduce Blush. Well, as dinner was being prepared I started getting a little nervous. I had the whole butterflies in my stomach, nauseated to the point of hyperventilation. When I started to talk with Isabelle, I found an instant friend at that moment and a sense of calm came over me. I was very comfortable around her and I thought that that in itself was a little odd. I had never really talked with her that much, but I'll never forget the first time I met her. I was coming out of the staff kitchen just before the overnight and I heard a little voice with a thick French accent, and at the table were Isabelle and Brandi after a hard day's work of the cowgirl sort. Immediately I approached the table and asked the obvious:

"Tu parles francais?"

"Oui."

"Vien d'ou?"

"Quebec."

And there wasn't much said after that. But as I stood there at the staff overnight speaking in both French and English with this girl, I knew there was something special about her but I couldn't put my finger on it — or at least not that night. Now I was confused, what do I do? I had planned to chase Blush that night but then everything changed. I found myself intrigued and delighted to talk with this girl, and little did I know at that time that she was going to change my life forever. Perhaps I had better explain the change later, as it does not entirely pertain to summer camp but it does to the Monte and Isabelle affair. I knew Ringo (appropriately given considering his large nipples and nipple rings) was interested in Isabelle, but I wasn't sure how much so I decided not to enter uncharted water until I knew more about the situation. As supper was being prepared we had noticed that the walkers had arrived sans Mad Dog (If you have ever seen a mad dog before there isn't anything else that needs to be said). She had decided to walk up by herself without a radio or anything, and we were all starting to get a little worried. A couple of the guys who knew the area decided to go and look for her. Everyone was getting worried and uptight about how this could have happened, and some people, I'm sure, wanted to point the blame at others, but I disagree and was just glad that Mad Dog was found. Well, she probably would have climbed the mountain if she felt like it, curse her endless energy and spunk. When she arrived, everyone was glad and the matter was soon forgotten.

We sat around the campfire that night and decided to pass around one of Beanie's (Beanie Baby Queen of the West) Beanie Babies (it was the moose in case you wanted to remember) and deliver anecdotes about where we were from and whatever else you could believe possible. It was a time for the staff to hobnob and mingle or whatever. I seemed to be more focused on Isabelle that night and almost forgot about Blush — I put her on the back burner that night. Even though she burned the gloves I had lent her when she was cold. Well, at least it wasn't Wings' (nickname derived itself from the Boeing 747 jet wings he had for hair) shoes. I was having a great time and when we put on our bracelets (I burned my fingertips pushing Blush's together — no matter what I did I never seemed to attract that girl). When all was said and done we headed off for bed and I went to say goodnight to the girls' tent and Darte (the nice way of saying Dirty) asked me to — no that would be lying — ordered:

"Show me your ass."

Well, I didn't want to disappoint, so I went to the boys' tent and rounded up a couple of volunteers. Cheeks (gee, I wonder where he got his name) and Snooze (the only guy I have ever known to sleep anywhere at anytime) willingly volunteered the use of their masculinity for the sheer entertainment of the women. Well, I received the nickname Monte after that episode. NO harm done. After that we returned to the tent for the night. It was pretty quiet, so I decided to open up the floor with:

"Anybody got any good jokes?"

I'm pretty sure Tex delivered the elephant joke that got the place rolling. It goes a little something like this (apply Tex's voice here):

"There was this elephant…Dirty joke…,"

Immediately the tent erupted with laughter, but the most laughter seemed to be coming from Bobby Hill's (well when and if you ever meet him, you know) direction. I never saw a guy laugh so hard before. Granted it's a great joke but a good five minutes later Bobby was still laughing, but it almost sounded like he was crying. Someone turned to Bobby and said:

"Bobby are you laughing?"

"Maybe."

I have to tell you that was one the funniest things in pre-camp, just the way Bobby laughs is very contagious.

When we awoke and made the long trek back to camp, I had great feeling in me. I felt like this was going to be a great summer, but little did I know it was going to be my greatest summer.

As pre-camp dwindled into first session, I was becoming concerned with the amount of salt Blush was consuming. It was not in moderation at all, you could have salted half of Highway 40 in the middle of winter with the amount of salt she was using. It would kill anyone over the age of forty. I turned and said what any concerned potential boy-toy-friend would say.

"Blush, that is not healthy."

"I know but I love salt so much," she said.

"Why? It's so salty."

"I know I should cut back," she said after retrieving her lunch from the bottom of the salt pile.

"You should really think about it because it is going to be a problem later on in life."

"I've been meaning to quit."

"Oh really, how is that? By taking in so much salt that your body starts producing it on its own in mass quantities?"

"No, cold turkey."

This was music to my ears. I knew that Blush was a competitor from way back in pre-camp when we played B-Ball. "You cannot," I said.

"I can too quit."

"Blush, let's be honest, you cannot quit cold turkey and you know it."

"Yes I can."

"Oh, really? Then you should have no problem making a bet on that. Should you put your money where your mouth is?"

"What did you have in mind?"

I have to admit this was shrewd, sly and classless all in the same breath. Note to self: none of the above.

"OK, if I catch you eating salt, then you are going to have to go swimming in the pond in your birthday suit."

"Fine, that is no problem."

That was the end of that and later that night I made sure every guy at camp knew what had transpired earlier that day.

On the last day of pre-camp I boarded the plane with Wookie (she came to camp with the nickname but at that time she had her own Neuf — I think she still does), Ginger (don't really remember why she got her nickname and she quit after session 1), Hamlet (given to him because he came from a town of thirty-eight people therefore his town is classified as a hamlet), Nova (he arrived late at pre-camp and would later coin the phrase DOOOOIT! He's also from Nova Scotia), Blush and myself. Hamlet, Blush and Nova were headed for Halifax to see what's to spare and if there's nothing there then Toronto, which is where Wookie, Ginger and I headed. I had a nice quiet time in Toronto with my grandparents and the rest of my family in southern Ontario. I'll reconvene here next chapter on my birthday, June 22, 1998, the first day of session 1.

Until we read it again.

Love, Monte

I wrote this when I was twenty years old and didn't finish much to my disappointment. The next three years of my life would involve me working with children at camp and it made me realise that teaching would be my career and my passion. I owe everything to Pits for taking a chance on me, and the friends that I made were life long. I don't know what I would have done if Tim Horton's didn't come to my rescue.

Chapter Two

Katimavik and Meeting Matthieu

Written by Matthieu and Anny Gagnon

Matthieu and Anny

Je me souviens encore très bien de ma première rencontre avec mon chum Matt, il y a plus de 20 ans. Fin des années 90, jeune adulte, mais encore avec l'attitude nonchalante d'un éternel adolescent. Je venais de terminer l'école secondaire et j'avais beaucoup de difficulté à relever le défi de me trouver un métier. J'avais beau chercher et tenter de me projeter dans le futur, je n'avais pas la moindre idée de quoi faire de ma peau. Heureusement, j'ai eu cette belle opportunité de participer à un programme qui pouvait m'aider à sortir de ma torpeur. J'ai sauté sur l'occasion. Première étape, Vernon (BC) pour entamer une aventure de 9 mois avec une bande de couillons comme moi, qui venaient des quatre coins du pays. Je ne suis même plus capable de me souvenir de tous les noms des membres de notre gang: Dick, BJ, Leslie, Darren, Evelyne? Merde je n'ai pas de mémoire. Cependant, j'ai énormément de souvenirs avec Matt. Il faut dire que nous avons cliqués ensemble dès les premières secondes de notre rencontre. On est des Matt, amoureux du Canadien de Montréal, c'était un match parfait!

J'avais 9 mois pour apprendre l'anglais et trouver des intérêts et aptitudes utiles dans la vie d'un adulte. J'ai commencé par expérimenter l'infographie avec la mise en page de photos du magazine Maxim sur les murs de ma chambre. Toute une œuvre d'art! Pas besoin de vous dire que Matt était mon cochambreur. Je me souviens des longues discussions avant de tomber endormi souvent aux petites heures du matin. Moi qui parle en français et Matt qui me répond en anglais, c'était les premières leçons.

Je suis arrivé à Vernon avec 500,00$ en poche et un petit livre de recueil que j'avais pour mission de remplir de souvenir. En trois semaines, j'avais bu pour 500,00$ de pichets de bière au Boston Pizza, seul, face à ce livre dans lequel j'ai souvent écrit vouloir retourner à la maison. Je me souviens du soir où j'ai bu les derniers dollars et que je parlais miraculeusement mieux l'anglais que le français. De retour vers la maison, ou je voulais seulement aller rejoindre mes copines de Maxim, j'ai dû faire face à notre project leader, la responsable de notre groupe, dont j'ai évidemment oublié le nom, qui m'attendait patiemment. On a eu une longue discussion et la conclusion fut quand même brutale. J'avais la nuit pour décider si je prenais un billet d'avion pour Montréal le lendemain matin. Eh bien je suis resté et la raison principale c'était Matt. Je ne pouvais quand même pas lui faire ça.

Je n'ai jamais regretté ma décision. Les mois suivants ont été parmi les plus beaux de ma vie. Moi qui pensais devenir un adulte, j'ai été adolescent plus que jamais! Tellement, qu'on n'a pas réussi à compléter les neuf mois initialement prévus. On écrivait l'histoire, en étant parmi les seuls à se faire montrer la porte du programme. Dommage, je crois encore aujourd'hui qu'on ne méritait pas un tel sort. On était des imbéciles heureux et sans prétention.

Quand j'ai vu Matt pour la dernière fois à Sturgeon Falls, j'ai apporté une photo de notre bonhomme de neige construit en face de la maison à Baie St-Paul. On avait arraché un morceau de la clôture du voisin pour y construire un immense pénis. Je me souviens encore de notre project leader qui nous suppliait de bien vouloir lui couper ce membre. Après tout ce travail, nous avions bien sûr refusé. Ça aussi c'était de l'art. Nous avions entamé notre cours séjour à Baie-St-Paul en force quand le soir de notre arrivée, nous avions accroché à sa porte de chambre, une poupée gonflable que nous avions équipée d'une banane dans l'entrejambe et d'une pince sur un toton. Une œuvre d'art! Quel choc elle a eu! Le ton était donné.

J'ai passé des mois fabuleux avec mon chum Matt à un moment clé de ma vie. Moment où je suis évidemment devenu un adulte.

Peu de temps après Katimavik j'ai déménagé dans mon premier appartement. Je quittais la maison avec mon amoureuse qui partage toujours ma vie aujourd'hui, deux enfants plus tard. C'est dans cet appartement qu'Anny a rencontré Matt, venu nous visiter avec Épiphanie, sa conjointe de l'époque et Hershey, son ami le plus fidèle. Cette boule de poils de suivait partout. Jusqu'à Bahreïn! Matt l'aimait inconditionnellement. On s'en souvient encore! à son image, Hershey était un chien chaleureux, facile, accueillant, authentique, sincère, fidèle. Matt était bon pour garder le contact avec ses amis. Il est venu nous visiter à plusieurs reprises au fil du temps malgré ses nombreux déplacements, en raison de son travail. À chacune de ses visites, Matt tenait toujours à s'occuper d'au moins un souper. Il a toujours cuisiné pour nous. Je me souviens de plats indiens et de son fameux gâteau au fromage. Matt était vraiment facile à recevoir, toujours de bonne humeur et le réservoir plein d'une énergie positive dont lui seul avait le secret.

Anny et moi avons choisi la journée la plus chaude de tout l'été 2007 pour nous marier et Matt avait réussi à organiser son horaire pour faire partie de la fête. Sur cent cinquante personnes présentes, il connaissait que nous deux et mes parents et pourtant plusieurs de mes amis se souviennent très bien de lui. Il s'est tellement bien intégré à la famille, qu'il a fini par baiser une des filles d'honneur dans les toilettes de la salle de réception. De toute beauté! Mon mariage est certainement l'une des journées les plus importantes de ma vie et Matt en a fait partie. Nous conserverons à jamais l'image de lui cette journée-là, une bière à la main. Heureusement qu'il était là le lendemain pour prendre soin d'Anny! Je devais aller m'occuper de ma famille alors descendu du Lac St-Jean, mais Matt e et Anny sont restés à la maison, question de récupérer un peu. Gaterade et soupe Lipton: il avait la recette gagnante de son bonheur! Peu de temps après, mais après beaucoup d'hésitation, il quitta le Canada, en direction de Moscou. Quelle bonne décision il aura prise!

Pour nous présenter Gemma, la femme de sa vie, Matt avait proposé un point de rencontre à Pembroke pour une fin de semaine. On a joué à la pétanque, au poker et bu du scotch toute la fin de semaine. Je me souviens encore de la bouteille que j'avais achetée au LCBO, un Laphroing quarter cask. On jouait dans le gazon, directement sur le terrain du B and B. On a passé la fin de semaine à se conter des histoires et à se taquiner. C'était notre spécialité. Si j'avais la chance, je profiterais de l'occasion pour lui rappeler en toute humilité, comment j'étais dominant à la pétanque. ;)

Gemma est donc entrée dans nos vies en toute simplicité. Après tout, nous avions un point commun: Matt! Dès les premiers instants, nous avions l'impression de nous connaître depuis toujours.

Anny et moi adorons New York et nous y sommes allez à plusieurs reprises, mais quand je pense à cette ville, je pense à Matt et Gemma. Quelle belle idée de se marier aux beaux milieux de Central Park. Il y a une fébrilité et une énergie vraiment spéciale qui émane d'un groupe de personnes réunies en voyage pour célébrer l'amour de deux personnes importantes dans nos vies. L'endroit de la célébration était magique, sous un petit pont sur lequel une bande de curieux s'était attroupée pour regarder la cérémonie. Au moment d'embrasser la mariée, la foule au-dessus de nos têtes s'est mise à applaudir et à scander des mots d'encouragements pour les nouveaux mariés. C'était comme dans un film. La photo la plus significative pour Anny, qui représente le plus Matt selon elle, vient de ce voyage.

C'était à la fin du mois de décembre et nous avons célébré la nouvelle année sur un bateau de croisière à regarder les feux d'artifice sur la rivière Hudson. Je pense encore souvent à cette soirée magique quand je bois un verre de mousseux dans les coupes à champagne que nous avons subtilement ramenées avec nous. Gemma avait la tête sortie de la limousine pendant tout le trajet de retour et parlait à tout le monde sur la rue comme si c'était une vedette internationale. La vie était moins glorieuse le lendemain matin lorsque son seul interlocuteur était la toilette de sa chambre d'hôtel:)

Nous ne sommes jamais allés à Singapour malgré les très nombreuses invitations de Matt. Il a même essayé de nous convaincre en nous disant qu'il avait une piscine. Il avait épuisé ces arguments rendu-là, je crois... Mais avec les enfants en bas âge, ce n'était pas possible de faire le voyage.

Mis à part le temps vécu avec Matt à Katimavik,il y a toujours eu une distance physique entre Matt et nous, mais cette distance n'a jamais été un obstacle. Et bien qu'on pouvait passer des mois sans se parler, notre amitié n'a jamais été altérée. Nous étions des amis au-delà la distance, au-delà du temps qui passait. Matt faisait partie de notre vie même s'il était loin. Il continuera d'en faire partie, là où il se trouve aujourd'hui. Avant de partir, il nous a remercier pour toutes les aventures. C'est lui, pourtant, qui nous en a fait vivre. Love you Fat Ass.

Chapter Three

Why I Loved Teaching

Written by Andrea Barry, Amy Long and Amber Smith-Comé

Amber Smith-Comé

In all of the conversations that I had with Matt over the years about teaching, I don't recall ever asking him why he became a teacher. Maybe it's because he was just so naturally a teacher that I never thought to ask. I think that most people become teachers because they love children and want to make a difference in children's lives, and I know that this was definitely true of Matt, but when I really think about why Matt loved teaching, I think that it was because he was so passionate about learning himself. This passion for learning made Matt an incredible and inspiring teacher who worked so hard to instill a love for learning in the students he taught. Matt loved to experience new things and then share that learning with those he cared about and those he taught. From history and math, books, cultures and customs, music, cooking, baking, sports and even knitting, Matt learned... and then he so generously shared, giving others the opportunity to learn through his experiences and adventures.

I think that Matt also loved teaching because it kept him young at heart and allowed him to stay a kid himself in so many ways. I asked some of his former students what they remembered most about having Mr. Dean as a teacher, and they all said that he made learning fun and interesting. One student shared a memory of sitting in class one day and hearing screaming kids outside in the schoolyard and then seeing Mr. Dean in full sprint with a rubber chicken in his hand, being chased by a pack of students. Another remembered learning about fractions through a rap song that Mr. Dean taught them, and him bringing his guitar to school to play in class. And yet another student fondly remembers how he introduced them to different world cultures with his souvenirs and memorabilia from his world travels and teaching abroad.

I will always remember and cherish the year that he and I team taught Grade 7/8 math. I think he spent just as much time teaching me that year as we did teaching the students. He definitely changed my thinking towards math learning, and it helped me to become a more confident math teacher at the intermediate level where I was most uncomfortable. I was able to see first hand how patient and understanding Matt was as a teacher. He not only was able to ignite a fire in his students, he also was able to excite his peers about teaching and about being able to connect with our students. He was an inspiration for me, and I am so grateful to have had that experience teaching and learning with him.

Whatever it was that inspired Matt to become a teacher, I am so glad it did because it led him to St. Anne School and into my life as a colleague and a friend. I learned so much from Matt, about teaching, about learning, about friendship, and about life and I, like all of the students who were so lucky to have had him as a teacher, will continue to be inspired by and learn from the lessons he taught.

Matt has been all around the world and left his imprint in every place he has been. His spirit lives on through everyone he touched in some way, and it definitely lives on at St. Anne School and in the community. The people he impacted here in Iroquois Falls will always remember Matt for his love of life, love of teaching and his dedication to his students and their learning.

Amy Long

It was around March of 2012 and Matt and I were in the teacher's lounge sorting out a huge assortment of rocks to get them ready for a provocation for our Sharing the Planet unit. I would pick up a rock and stare at it having no idea, and Matt would look up from his rock, tell me what type of rock I was holding, tell me how he could tell, and then get back to his pile. After about three of these conversations, I eyed him with suspicion. It was then that he told me before studying education at university, he was enrolled in geology. I could not stop laughing… Rocks! Since that evening, I will pick up a rock and, at times, be able to identify it. If not I think, *Matt would know,* and smile in disbelief at the fact he was almost a geologist. He was also courted by CSIS, the Canadian version of the CIA or MI6. So, for a while it looked like Matt's career was going to be a spy or rocks.

Then he became a camp counsellor and everything changed. Matt and I talked about camp…a lot! We agreed you could always tell a camp person a mile away. Matt's camp experience was different to mine. He never went to camp as a child; he applied to be a counsellor at one of the Tim Horton Foundation camps. These camps are for low income families. He noticed a vast difference from his childhood to that of some of his campers. He decided that helping children was what he needed to do. He switched his major to education and became a teacher.

Matt and I started teaching Grade 2 at the Canadian International School at the same time. He with several years of teaching experience under his belt and I…well, I was in the final leg of my postgraduate diploma for education. I have always said that Matt didn't have a choice in our friendship — it was forced upon him by me bursting into his room daily with my planner saying, "So…What are we doing tomorrow?" If there were other things on this plate or he was annoyed at the intrusion, I never knew it. He would sit patiently at his desk, ask questions and guide me through it. He was always teaching.

In all of the time we spent teaching, planning and hanging out together, I cannot recall ever having a conversation about why he loved teaching. We did have several that showcased his teaching philosophy. When it came right down to it, everything flew out the window when it came to helping a student achieve success: "You do whatever the child needs to get them to where they need to go." And he would. He would work tirelessly and patiently: guiding, conferencing, coming at things from different ways. If a child needed more practice time, he gave it. If a child needed encouragement, he gave it. Every year he created an environment that was fair, supportive and fun. His students knew what to expect, and they loved learning with him. He went above and beyond, and that is why the parents loved him.

He did all of it because he loved teaching. It was who he was. He would glow with pride when his students succeeded. He loved the look on a child's face when everything finally clicked. He loved hearing their ideas and thoughts. He loved guiding their learning, helping them, believing in them and celebrating their successes with them. I think he loved giving all children a taste of what he had with his mom and siblings because he knew from his camp experience not everyone has a safe, fair, supportive, caring place with someone who is on their side, who wants the best for them. I think he loved all the moments: the fun, maddening, loud, funny, at times crazy, awesome moments. But I think he loved the quiet moments most of all; those ones when his student would look at him, smile and quietly say, "Mr. Dean…I get it."

Andrea Barry

Matt told me that he never knew that he wanted to be a teacher. In fact, he wasn't really sure what he wanted to be (other than a professional hockey player, of course). One summer, he found himself working as a camp counsellor at the Tim Horton Children's Ranch in Kananaskis, Alberta. He told me that when he first arrived there, he didn't know anyone. He didn't know anything about being a camp counsellor — no songs, nothing. He was so nervous.

But that first experience at THCR changed his life forever. That year, he got to work with children from some really disadvantaged backgrounds. This made him feel so lucky to have grown up with the loving mom, and loving brothers and sister that he had. It was while he was at camp that he said to himself, "This is it. This is what I want to do with the rest of my life." That was when Matt decided to be a teacher.

He spent a few summers at THCR and was ready to go back for a final summer when he found out that he had been accepted to the JET

Programme. JET is the Japan Exchange and Teaching Programme. It is a programme that is sponsored by the Japanese Government. It offers Canadian teachers the opportunity to work as a teacher in Japan. Matt could not wait to get started! His JET Programme experience launched his career as an international educator!

I am not exactly sure of the timeline, but at some point Matt got his teacher's certification, worked in the Canadian public school system, and then took a leave of absence from his job to teach in Moscow. In Moscow, Matt taught Grade 4. At this school, he also met a beautiful Grade 3 teacher named Gemma — and you know how that story ends! I first met Matt when he joined the Canadian International School in Singapore.

When Matt and Gemma first arrived at CIS, they had some pretty unique jobs. Gemma was the Head of Aquatics, running our enormous aquatics programme. Our school was growing quickly and we needed another open minds teacher, and another drama teacher, but did not have enough students to warrant a full additional teaching load for either of these positions. So Matt was given the job of open minds/drama teacher. Now, what you have to understand is that these positions were very charismatically driven by the current teachers (Carolyn, the drama teacher, and Franklyn, the open minds co-ordinator). Franklyn and Carolyn both spent time with Matt trying to show them how best to do their (his) job! Matt was so good about it, saying, "I can only be myself!" And he tried really hard to facilitate these two programmes alongside Carolyn and Franklyn. But Matt's time as open minds/drama teacher was not to last long....

Matt started at CIS in August, but by October things were going DOWN in the Grade 2 team! I was the lead teacher of the Grade 2 team at the time. One of the Grade 2 teachers was let go rather abruptly in October, and Matt was asked to step in and take over this class. Matt was told about two weeks in advance that he would be taking over a classroom, but we needed him to keep it confidential and we could not tell him which class he would be taking over. Can you imagine?

On the day before the October break, the Grade 2 teacher was quietly told his contract was over and Matt was told whose class he would be taking over. He took a deep breath and was like, "Okay!!!!" Together, Matt and I packed up the other teacher's classroom, and I helped him to set it up for himself to begin following the October break. Once again, he was stepping into a programme that was rather charismatically driven, as the teacher that had been let go was BELOVED by staff, parents and students. Many were very upset that they had a new teacher in the classroom.

But Matt just showed up with his easy-going and welcoming attitude and smiling face. He quickly won over everyone with his professionalism, work ethic and a love for kids. You could regularly find him in the classroom during break times, working to provide students who needed it with additional support. He was a casual guy in terms of his personal style, and so regularly chose to wear a CIS school shirt rather than a stuffy button-up dress shirt. He had a clothes rack in his classroom — hanging on it a dress shirt and a collection of CIS shirts.

I have to tell you that at our Celebration of Life for Matt, held at CIS, many former students and parents showed up to shed tears and share stories. Matt can rest knowing that he truly made a difference in the lives of families, children and teachers that he worked with. I later became vice principal of the primary school at CIS, and held this position for five years. Every single year, I had parents come to my office requesting Matt Dean to be their child's teacher. I would go as far as to say that he was the most requested teacher in the school.

Matt not only shared his love of learning with his students, but he also shared his love for hockey. He played each week in a staff floor hockey league at the school. During recess, he helped supervise pick-up games of ball hockey in our bus bay. He was a hockey coach for our hockey co-curricular activity (IN SINGAPORE, where it is about 35 degrees Celsius each day) AND he ended up coaching the Singapore National Hockey Team! His dream of going pro (as a coach!) came true in Singapore. Matt gave 100% to everything he did.

In all of the ways that Matt was a spectacular teacher, he was also a spectacular colleague and friend. As a team, we regularly shared snacks and hung out together. He was thoughtful, caring, friendly and SO FUNNY. When Matt's ALS diagnosis was shared with the CIS school community, over $250,000 was raised within a year to support the Dean family. Everyone wanted to help. This is a testament to the kind of teacher and member of the CIS community that he was. He is dearly missed.

Chapter Four

University Days

Written by Greg Callan

The year was 1999 and I was about to start my first year at Laurentian University in Sudbury, Ontario. Matt had already completed his first year in the anthropology program at Laurentian and had become friends with Mindy, a girl I had been dating since high school. Mindy introduced us and we hit it off instantly. Matt had just gotten back into town after the summer and was in between residences. Simply put, he was homeless and looking for a place to live off campus for the year. I was working front desk at a little dive called the Sorrento Motel and since we had already become best friends, I offered him a place stay. As glamorous as that might sound, the reality was Matt slept on the floor in a sleeping bag behind the front desk while I worked the graveyard shift. In the morning, Matt would wake up just before 7 a.m., clean up his stuff and wait in my car until I was relieved by the person who worked the 7-3 shift. Then we would go look for apartments for him. This lasted for about a week or so until we were able to find Matt a nice basement apartment close enough where he was able to walk to Laurentian. Why he didn't just sleep at my house the nights I worked I don't know. I guess subconsciously we knew it would make for a great story. A twenty-year friendship full of fun stories and experiences.

The years continued to pass and Matt would start travelling the world, teaching in Japan, the Middle East, Russia and Singapore. While

Matt was doing all of these awesome things, I finished teacher's college and started my own teaching career just outside of Toronto, Ontario.

Throughout all of this time, Matt and I kept in touch and he would tell me about all of his adventures in the countries he was teaching in at the time. Matt could write a book just on those experiences alone. One thing about our relationship that I always valued was that no matter how much time passed that we didn't see each other or talk, or how many thousands of kilometers separated us, when we connected it was as if no time had passed at all. We always picked up right where we left off, reminiscing about university and reliving the memories and experiences that we had shared together.

I always envied the way Matt lived his life travelling all over the world and learning about the cultures he had immersed himself in. On many occasions Matt would encourage me to come with him to whatever country he was hitting next. Of course, I wanted to go. Who wouldn't? These were experiences of a lifetime! However, there were always responsibilities and commitments that prevented me from taking that leap with Matty.

It is now the end of 2006 and Matt comes to me with another opportunity to teach overseas, this time in Russia. Matt wanted me to come with him and while it sounded amazing to travel the world with my best friend, I was hesitant as I had my son, Nicholas, to think about. Matt understood that leaving Canada for a year would be difficult. However, that wasn't the only thing holding me back. You see, there was this girl. I know what you're thinking: Isn't it always about a girl? I had met someone special that I had started seeing at the time. I explained to Matt that I had met this awesome girl named Julia Compton. She was super-hot, funny and smart. The relationship was still in its early stages, but I was also reluctant to leave because I wanted to see where this relationship with Jules could go. Needless to say, I stayed and Jules and I eventually got married in August of 2011, had two beautiful children of our own and built an amazing life together as a family of five in Burlington, Ontario. It looks like I made the right decision.

Matt's decision to go to Russia turned out to be a great decision for him also. During that year in Russia, Matty met and fell in love with a young woman from England. That wonderful young lady, of course, turned out to be Gemma Wolfe. Jules and I instantly fell in love with Gemma, her sense of humour and the way she could put Matty in his place. There was something about her accent and the way she used British slang to tell him off when he was being a jerk. We also saw how happy they were together and the strong love that was developing between the two of them.

The duo of Matt and Greg had now become a foursome. A foursome that shared so many laughs and inside jokes; Gemma and Matt moving to Singapore to teach at the International School there, two weddings (ours and theirs), and four amazing kids — ours (Lucy and Felix), and theirs (Carter and Harry). Matt and Gemma were always the ones to call and see how we were doing and to tell us about the latest addition to our Joke Book. It is a book full of sarcastic comments and jokes the four of us had made during nights playing games, eating countless dinners, drinking beer and wine, and of course watching our favourite movie, *Step Brothers* — a movie that came to symbolize our relationship as a foursome. A relationship that was fun, silly, loving and supportive.

Over the next five years we continued to form new memories together. The anticipation of Matt and Gemma finally coming home to settle in Canada with their family was dampened when we found out that Matt had been going through tests because of symptoms he was experiencing that were identical to ALS. Ultimately, Matt would be diagnosed with this terrible disease. The only word that comes to mind would be shock when Matt told me the news. I didn't know what to say, and I felt so helpless. I could only imagine what Matt and Gemma were going through.

Matt has been a special person, not only in my life but in the lives of many others. He will always be in my heart and not a day goes by that I don't think about him. I'm going to close this chapter with a reference from *Step Brothers*:

"After that courageous act Matt, the one I call Nighthawk, showed me by sleeping on the floor of that run-down dive of a motel they call the Sorrento, I knew, maybe, just maybe, someday we could become friends. Friends who ride majestic, translucent steeds, shooting flaming arrows across the bridge of Hemdale. I would follow Nighthawk into the mists of Avalon."

I'm honoured to have known Matt and grateful for our friendship. I love you man.

Chapter Five

Moscow

I had a happy childhood and was raised in a great town that always felt like home. The 80s may have been the greatest decade to be a kid ever. We had it all — cool music, fashion, toys, video games and most importantly the freedom to roam and play outside with minimal parental interference... I mean parental supervision. We had sleepovers in shelters/teepees/cabins that we built, usually without the help of our parents, all summer long. We went fishing and swimming in the lake. It was awesome. I want to thank all of the people of our town that helped shape my life in a positive way, and I am sure that others would agree. I would like to thank the Adams, Alkins, Barbers Barkers, Beans, Bordens, Brochus, Brooks, Campbells, Champagnes, Danihers, Davises, Demilles, Elliots, Gravelles, Guilmettes, Hannahs, Howards Madigans, Milnes, Nautas, Ransoms, Wilsons and Wilkinsons.

I am a huge hockey fan and a large portion of my childhood was dedicated to it. We were always playing on the outdoor rink or street hockey in my hometown. Rain, snow or shine, you would find us outside pretending to be the hockey heroes of our day. Gretzky, Lemieux, Orr, Deanov and Barkerov. Okay, the last two are really our last names with ov added to the end. We grew up during the intense Canada vs. USSR rivalry. So, naturally we took turns playing this out in our own ways. Did we ever have some real nail-biters.

So what does this have to do with Moscow exactly? Long story short, I was granted a leave of absence from my teaching job in Canada so I could work in Moscow. Everyone said that I was going to end up coming back to Canada with a Russian wife. Well, they were half right.

I sold my house and prepared to move to the other side of the world knowing nothing about what I was getting myself into. I packed up my clothes and prepared my dog for the long trip to Mother Russia. I paid off my debt from the house proceeds — just an important detail that I realised when I was diagnosed and the screaming in my mind about finances took hold. I took Hershey everywhere, and this was going to be country number three for him (Canada, Bahrain and Russia). Hershey was a cross between a German shorthaired pointer and a black lab and came out looking like a sleek, muscular chocolate lab. He was an excellent traveller. He was always treated with the utmost care while in the hands of the airlines that I chose to fly with. If you are ever considering travelling with your pet I highly recommend for travel inside Canada either Air Canada or WestJet. For international flights I would suggest KLM, Aeroflot and Czech Airlines. Hershey always made the flights with a wag in his tail and a skip in his step. Often I received him before my luggage as was the case in Moscow. He was brought to me as soon as I cleared security. Another important tip for travelling with your dog is to have a veterinarian help you at your destination. I always did that, and I never regretted it.

Quick side story. The veterinarian I hired was also the one responsible for looking after the dogs of foreign dignitaries when they arrived in Moscow. She told me that I had done all of my paperwork correctly, which is a big deal in Russia. You are guaranteed to do paperwork. Just how bad is it if you don't do the paperwork correctly? Ask the person responsible for President Obama's military service dogs. Someone didn't do it and the dogs were not allowed into Russia, but being the president of the United States of America carries a certain amount of sway . So my next piece of advice is to double check your forms.

Moscow is an amazing city, and it should be on everyone's travel list. Rich in culture, history and architectural beauty, I love this town and it loves me. I love Moscow not only for the people I met and had the privilege of working with, but because I met the love of my life there. Gemma and I worked at the same campus. She taught Grade 3 and I taught Grade 4. We did not hit it off right away, and I believe she thought I was a grumpy fucker. I have one of those serious faces but how I am/was perceived has never really bothered me.

Who am I trying to kid? Of course it did.

But those who get to know me, know I am not a grumpy fucker but a funny fucker. Gemma and I started dating kind of in October 2008. Our first kind of date was to a recommended pizza place. We found the restaurant quite easily and were sat at a cozy table. Gemma looked lovely in her sweater and slacks…I don't really remember what she was wearing, but I know that she looked beautiful and I felt like I could be myself with her. The waitress brought the menu, and it was in Russian. Not one word of English anywhere. So we ordered by pointing at the menu randomly and hoping for the best. We ended up with some kind of calzone that turned out to be not too bad. Then I took Gemma back to her apartment and made my way back to my apartment to look after Hershey. Did we kiss? Wouldn't you like to know. A gentleman never kisses and tells.

We had a school break in October and when Gemma came back from England, we decided to make things more official. We started dating exclusively on the 5th of November. I knew Gemma was special when I met her, but I never knew how special until we went on holiday together to Scotland just after Christmas. We were invited to spend New Year's with my friends, Gavin and Clare (two of the most amazingly kind and wonderful people on earth), and a bunch of their friends. Gemma flew to Aberdeen from Bristol, and I flew in from Oslo where I was visiting my great friend, Carl, and his wife, France. We met at the airport and picked up the car we had rented. I had printed out the directions to where we were going on MapQuest. Yep, I said MapQuest. Trying to find Logie Coldstone during the day is not that easy and we did it at night time and without any issues. Gemma drove since we were in the UK and they drive on the opposite side of the road, the weirdos… just kidding. Gemma has always done the driving anywhere we have gone where they drive on the left. Gemma is an excellent driver and navigator, and I always enjoyed our trips together.

When we arrived in Logie Coldstone we met everyone and turned in for the night. Over the next few days we took in the mesmerising Scottish scenery and grew closer together as a couple. I look at that trip as the point when Gemma and I really connected and I knew in my heart that we were meant for each other.

Falling in love with Gemma is not all I did that first year in Moscow. I flooded a local police department, made my friends go "This coincidence is mind-blowing ," moved in with Gemma after her apartment was burgled and played hockey with some friends of the government and another group of guys that were excited to have a Canadian join in their weekly game. Oh, and I was invited to a 50th birthday party of a UUSR hockey legend, which was a who's who of Russian society. He may have been responsible for Canada winning the 1987 Canada Cup!

The Flood

The flooding of the police station is funny now, but I was brickin it at the time of the first pound on the door. You see, earlier in the day I had decided to go to Izmailovo Market and do some shopping for some souvenirs and get some shaslik. I decided to put a load of laundry on so when I got back I could hang it up to dry. When I eventually got home later that day, I noticed a small puddle where my washing machine was in my bathroom. I thought that it must have leaked and no big deal. Then while I was checking around the washer just in case, I saw it. The hose to drain the machine had completely come off, and I was a little bit worried about where all the water had gone since there was barely a trace of it in my bathroom. Well, I was going to find out soon enough and pretty much drop a load in my shorts.

In the early evening, a strong pounding on my door threw Hershey basically into attack mode. I was a little bit worried that it was the people below who were probably pretty pissed with me. So I approached the door silently and peered through the peephole. There standing outside my apartment were two very angry police officers. I then knew it was the police station where the water had gone into. I debated with myself about opening the door and then the next thing I know is that I am opening the door with one hand and holding onto Hershey with the other. You should have seen the look of shock on their faces when I started apologizing in groveling English. At this point Hershey was going crazy, so much so that I was worried that they were going to draw their guns. They proceeded to tell me that I just missed the computers and the filing cabinets. They wanted to know about my purpose for being in Russia and why I was living in this apartment. Luckily I had my phone in my pocket and while they were asking me questions I pulled it out and called Maria, the school secretary. Maria was so much more than a secretary, she saved my bacon and always helped and worked beyond her pay grade. I was extremely grateful for her diffusing the situation entirely and translating everything in such a way that when they left they were pleasant.

Once the news of my interrogation made its way to the owner of the school, a friend was called. I am not sure exactly who, but the police never bothered me again and gave me a head nod whenever they saw me, which continued until I left.

The Coincidence

Well, I guess I will start with Nadine and Rossy, our closest friends in Moscow. They are amazing people who are always up for a great time and will be there for you when you need them the most. I first got to know Nadine since we worked for the same school but at different campuses a few blocks away from each other. Nadine and I got along straight away and started hanging out almost immediately. When I met Rossy it was as if I had met a long lost brother. We have similar senses of humour and I will include Nadine in that as well. We always had so much fun. So much so, I always chuckle inside when I think about them and it always puts a smile on my face.

So, to make a long story short, I was looking for a place to get hockey gear. I was explaining this to Nadine and Rossy one night, and Rossy asked me if it would be like broomball equipment. I said it could be. He told me that his boss wanted it out of the office and I got it for free. It was really everything that I needed but skates and gloves. I couldn't believe my good fortune but my Nonie always said that I could fall into a bucket of shit and come out smelling like a rose. This statement has held true to my life until my ALS diagnosis. There is no way to get the smell out. I told Rossy to thank his boss for me and thought no more about it until one night at La Roma.

We were out for dinner and drinks at La Roma, our local pizza place, that had arguably the best pizza in Moscow and awesome owners that always treated us well. So we were talking about my quest to play hockey somewhere in the city when Rossy came up with a great idea. He said that I should find a hockey bar and see what I could find out about joining a team. I thought that was a solid idea. The next words to come out of his mouth surprised me with a smile to another time in my life. He told me that his boss's wife worked for the F1 and there is an F1 bar, so there must be a hockey bar. I said, "Your boss's name must be Paul." I thought he was going to fall off of his chair. He was stunned and wanted to know how I knew his name.

You have to back track in time to when I lived in Bahrain three years earlier. Paul was my neighbor in Manama, someone who I got along with quite well, and the person who got Hershey out of quarantine by calling the prince. Paul was a guy that could do anything for a friend. I am so glad that he got Hershey out of quarantine. It was like a dirty doggy prison. Needless to say that this was not the only major coincidence to happen to me. It happened to me everywhere I went around the world.

The Meeting in the Lunchroom

As I was one of just a couple of Canadians working for the British International School of Moscow, I felt that it was my duty to take people to see a game. I hoped to convert some people to the church of hockey. I decided to write on the lunchroom whiteboard and see if there were any takers.

In walked Margarita, a very classy lady who looks out of place for a teacher's assistant. She saw what was written on the whiteboard and asked me if I knew anything about it. I confessed it was my idea, and she asked me if I liked hockey. I said that I am Canadian and I love it. She proceeded to ask me if I played growing up, and I recounted my earlier story at the beginning of the book. She told me about her husband and how he used to play. She said this in such a nonchalant way I had to think that based on her age that he definitely grew up during the reign of the Big Red Machine. I asked her where he played. She said he was pretty good, and I was curious about what that meant. Then she told me he won two gold medals at the Olympics. I am pretty sure that the expression on my face was just like a child at Christmas waiting to open a present. Well, Christmas came early in Moscow that year, and it was glorious. And Santa Claus was about to give me a gift of a lifetime.

Approximately a week later she asked me if I was busy for the upcoming weekend and I said I wasn't. She asked me if I would like to go to an old person game her husband was playing in. I knew that she meant old timers, and of course I said yes. I was super excited about the weekend, and I couldn't believe my good fortune. She told me to arrive just before one o'clock at the arena and meet her at the main entrance.

When the weekend finally arrived I could no longer control my excitement and I made sure to leave early so that I would not be late. I took the metro there just to make sure that I wasn't late. I really enjoyed taking the metro; it is an amazing display of human ingenuity and art, and I highly recommend that if you are ever considering visiting Moscow you spend a good portion underground. When I got to the arena there was no one to be found at the main entrance and it was locked. I double-checked my phone to make sure that I didn't have the time screwed up. According to my phone I was in the right place at the right time. I thought that maybe I was at the wrong entrance and decided to walk around the arena before I hit the panic button and called Margarita.

As I walked around the arena, I came across another entrance alright, but this one had soldiers with machine guns. As I approached the soldiers they asked me for my ticket, to which I replied in terrible Russian: "My friend is bringing it for me." They didn't really understand what I was saying, so I called Margarita to help me. Help me she did. One of the soldiers escorted me into the building and to the capable hands of a little usher. What I saw next took me by surprise. The arena was empty and from where I was standing there was no one to be found. Then the music started. The best I could understand was it was introduction music. Then the players skated out and lined up on the blue lines. Then they played and sang *Happy Birthday* while a brand new midnight black Lexus SUV was driven out for the guest of honour, which Margarita forgot to mention was her husband. It was his fiftieth birthday party, and he was being thanked by the government for his service to his country.

At the end of all of that, my phone rang. It was Margarita wondering where I was. I told her where I was in the rink and she came to get me. She brought me to where everyone was sitting, and it really was a who's who of Russian society and little me from Callander. There were so many famous people there that I was starstruck. Who were they? I can't tell for fear of my safety. Just kidding…or am I? I can tell you this: Sergei Makarov sat behind me. After the game I joined Margarita and her husband at his reception for food and champagne. The next thing I know, her husband is being given a stick like you get in the NHL after 1000 games. What a day!

What does this have to do with the '87 Canada Cup? It turns out that he was left off the team because he was fighting with Tikanov, who could be crusty on the best of days. He could have been the difference in those tight games and the difference between winning or losing. I'm glad I don't have to think about it because it was the best hockey ever played, period. I do feel bad for him not playing but respectfully glad he didn't or one of the greatest memories from my childhood would not exist. Sorry Mr. Kozhevnikov. After all this, I was invited to play weekly with some friends of the government and they were great and treated me like one of their own. I played almost every weekend and I had a ton of fun.

Gemma Was Burgled

I returned to Moscow before Gemma after we parted ways in Scotland. When Gemma arrived home she was to call me and I would bring her dinner. I didn't expect the panic in her voice when I answered her call. She was totally upset and rightly so. When she arrived at her apartment she noticed that the main door was unlocked, which is almost impossible when you look at the amount of locks there are. Before she could even finish explaining what was happening, I was already running towards her apartment. It took me less than ten minutes to get to her apartment. It normally was a forty-minute hike. I was bookin it to say the least. When I got there Gemma was crying, which is one of the only times I have seen her cry in our ten years together.

Her apartment was a total shambles. They took a majority of the valuables but left things like her Estée Lauder perfume that was unopened. One of the strangest things that was stolen was face cream that was already used. We were able to get a hold of someone from the school to help us deal with the police. When the police arrived, I was in awe. There were about five of them plus a dog. They dusted the whole apartment down and went door-to-door looking for leads. They didn't find anything. The school was great and gave Gemma the money to replace everything that was stolen. There was no way I would let Gemma return to her apartment, so she moved in with me, and the rest is history.

Moscow Year 2

Gemma and I spent the next year apart. It was difficult but exciting because I knew I had met my soulmate. Now I had to think about how I was going to hold on to her. So I got creative and I made sure that she knew I loved her. I continuously sent her things so she knew I was thinking about her and that I loved her. I just looked at it as a year apart; I looked at it as I went to work for a few months and went back to her. It wasn't easy at times, but I never doubted her or her smile and her sincerity. We were a match made in heaven. I had a great year in Moscow, and I enjoyed how everything worked out. Then when that time came to move back to Canada I had amazing memories of Russia and all the people I met there.

I played hockey with Russian people and it was fabulous. I was treated as an equal even when Canada spanked Russia at the Olympics. I was worried about going to the rink after that game, but when I arrived the men I played hockey with shook my hand. They even brought beer to celebrate. This is only one small fraction of the camaraderie and friendship I experienced with Russian people. It is not like you see on TV; everyone is just like everyone else. Trying to make ends meet, be kind, be a friend and friendly to those who are new to Russia.

Cocktails with Rossy and Nadine

Rossy and I got into making cocktails together, and often Nadine would be there helping out or drinking whatever we made. It was always great fun and we created the most amazing dessert cocktail called The Chocolate Tingle. The Chocolate Tingle is comprised of one pot of Danone vanilla yogurt with chocolate shavings and crunchy little chocolate balls, vodka, milk, and topped off with chili chocolate by Lindt. The only unfortunate part about this cocktail is that we never really nailed down the correct proportions. The first time we made it, it was delicious and amazing. But we never wrote down what we did and no matter how hard we tried we could not quite duplicate the first time. Maybe because we had already had a few, who knows?

Pool and Poker

Often some of the guys we worked with would play pool and poker. Our neighborhood pool hall was always busy, but usually only the Russian version of pool tables were busy. The common tables were usually free. This pool hall was always full of characters that you would not want to mess with. That being said, in Moscow you are fine as long as you mind your own business and don't get involved in what does not concern you. It sounds a little silly for this day and age but I found it to be refreshing. That might be odd to anyone reading this but spend some time there and it will make more sense.

One of my favourite things was when we played poker, it was always a culinary affair. I made my famous chili whenever I hosted. The other guys would take care of the food at their places. The games were always fun and full of beer. I won quite a few times as well as Big Al, a British guy who looked like Al MacInnis. Guess who gave him that nickname? He was also my roommate when Gemma went back home.

The Proposal

To my boys. This is where you get creative. For example, I really wanted to do something special for your mom so I decided to plan something amazing. I told your mom that I won a trip for two to Venice, Italy, in December 2009. But first I had to get the ring. Your mother had her heart set on a Tiffany Lucida engagement ring. I called all around the world to find her ring (Paris, New York, Toronto, London and Moscow). Luckily they had one at Heathrow. Once I got the ring I could put the plan into motion. I created everything that was needed — the pdf of the contest, fake email from the company, and I mailed the book to your mom that I won in the contest. Your mom had no idea what was happening. We made our way to the airport and when we arrived we learned that our flight was cancelled. Snow hit Italy and especially Venice. Your mother said, "Don't worry about it. It is a free trip, we don't have to go." Needless to say, I wasn't giving up. I was lucky enough to get a hold of a lady at BA who was a romantic. She put us on a flight the next day in business class. I phoned the hotel and they moved everything for us to match our flight times.

When we arrived at the airport the next day, the security guard ended up taking everything out of my bag, even the ring. This is the only time your mother ever saw me angry. Ask her to tell you the story. She spent the next two days asking me nonstop when I was going to ask her. It was the second night in Venice, and it was snowing. We were walking opposite the Santa Maria de la Salud and your mother looked radiant in her red jacket as the snow fell slowly through the night sky. I told your mom to look how beautiful the church looked as the snow swirled around it. I fumbled around in my pocket looking for the ring for what seemed like an eternity. I finally asked her and she said...yes! Make the same effort because who you want to spend the rest of your life with is someone who deserves your best.

Chapter Six

Back to Canada

Iroquois Falls Part 2

When my leave of absence was over, I returned to Iroquois Falls and taught Grade 5. This was my second stint in the Falls, and it was my last. I enjoyed my time there and made lifelong friends and memories. Gemma and I were still apart at this time and wouldn't be together full-time until we were married a year and a half later. It was also where Gemma would cut her teeth during her first Canadian winter. So what happened with me while I patiently waited for my love?

The school year went by in a blink of an eye and before I knew it, I was planning our wedding. You heard right, I planned almost our whole wedding in New York City. I did a pretty good job of it, if I do say so myself. The only real heart-wrenching moment I had been confronted with was the decision to put Hershey to sleep.

The Death of Hershey

Hershey was no ordinary dog. That is a bit of an understatement. He travelled more of the world than the average human being. We got Hershey during my last year of high school. He was a loveable scamp that could just about do anything and completely get away with it virtually unscathed. He could also pretty much eat whatever he wanted and would barely suffer the consequences either by myself or his body; he should have died according to the list of things that dogs should not eat, but he didn't, and he ate everything on that list. Like the time I came home from school and discovered that he had opened the cupboard where I kept the garbage can to feast on its contents. What were the contents, you ask? They were the remnants of twenty-four chicken wings a friend and I had the night before. What happened to him? A terrible case of the farts and not the nice kind. God, were they awful. You would think that after all of those bones, he should have died. Nothing food-related ever really caused him harm and it should have. A brain tumor ended up causing his death.

I remember his first seizure in the summer of 2011; we were at my mom's house in the basement and Hershey sneezed. He then started convulsing and his tongue was hanging out his mouth in a very limp state. As soon as the seizure stopped, I rushed him to our vet. Hershey had completely recovered by then, and the vet told me that it could be an isolated incident and to monitor him. It was in October that the seizures returned, and I couldn't let my best friend suffer through another round of seizures.

I phoned the veterinarian in Timmins to help me since it was the weekend and our local veterinarian in Iroquois Falls was closed. The whole forty-five-minute car ride I cried. Hershey was back to himself, so I put the back window down so that he could enjoy the fresh air blowing in his face one last time. When we arrived at the clinic, I didn't want to get out of the car because I knew it would be over. All of the good times and memories came flooding into my heart like a tidal wave of emotions that were trying to stop me. My brain, however, knew that the right thing to do was take him inside to end his suffering in the most painless way possible.

Eventually I worked up the courage to do it and with tears streaming down my face I walked to the back of my car and opened the tailgate. I scooped up Hershey in my arms and took him inside. The vet was very kind and lead me to the back room where I placed Hershey on the cold stainless steel table. He would not even try to get up, which is how I knew it was time. The vet offered a medication that might have prolonged his life but not necessarily his suffering. I decided to go ahead with putting him to sleep. I called everyone so they could say their goodbyes and tell him that they loved him. When that was done the vet prepared Hershey for the procedure. I held him tightly and I told him how much he meant to me and that I loved him with all my heart. About thirty seconds later, he was gone. The drive home was the loneliest I have ever had. I am still hurt when I think about it.

The Wedding

I wish that we could do it all over again. It was that amazing. We flew to New York on the 27th of December and organized things for the wedding. We had already taken care of the majority of the details before we arrived; when I say "we" I really mean "me." I handled about 90% of the planning because I wanted to make sure that Gemma got the wedding of her dreams.

We hired a car to drive us to our hotel. For us there was only one place to stay and that was the Waldorf. We stayed for a full week. And because we were getting married they upgraded us to a one bedroom suite with a fireplace. There was a bottle of champagne on ice in our room when we opened the door. We were also assigned an assistant to help us with anything else that we needed. I don't think I could say enough good things about The Waldorf, there are just too many. Hotel check! A big one!

We also created little information pages about the locations, times and menu…

Everything you need to know about
Matt and Gemma's Wedding Day!

Wedding Day Itinerary

1:50 – Guests to arrive at the Bethesda Terrace (See map for directions)

2:00 – Arrival of the bride! Wedding ceremony to begin.
2:20 – Time for some photos.

2:30 – Make our way over to Rockefeller Center for some ice-skating, snacks and a few drinks. (Remember to bring your skates if you have them!)

7:15 – Head to the Puttanesca restaurant for a delicious three course meal. Drinks (wine and beer) included. Please see the menu for choices.

10:30 – Time to say our goodbyes and head back to our hotels for the night.

The next day our friends and family started to arrive and as luck would have it, Nadine and Rossy were visiting her sisters and we could have a good catch up over some drinks. We met them at one of the oldest bars in the city. It was really cool. It was a shame that they could not stick around for the wedding, but they had to go back to England. They gave us all kinds of tips and advice on places to go while we were there. I don't remember the names of the places now, but I remember them as being fantastic. Her sister's husband's liquor store provided the champagne for the party that we had in our suite the night before our wedding. Then we went out for a bachelor dinner for me and a bachelorette dinner for Gemma. We ended up going to a restaurant just off Times Square. It was quite good, but the best was walking around Times Square smoking the giant cigars I got earlier that day.

My Eleven-Year-Old Nephew's Version

If you want to learn about the world, don't ask me. If you want to know about how wonderful travelling the globe is, don't ask me. If you want to know about anything but the immediate 100km around my house, don't ask me. I've only been outside of the country once. Perhaps that may change in the near future? Who knows. What I know is that the farthest I've ever left the comfort zone of my little North Bay, is a small town you may know as New York City.

It was a crisp December in the ever so farther away year of 2011. My uncle was getting married and he decided that a cold winter wonderland of a metropolis was the perfect place for such an occasion, and I'd have to agree with him. It wasn't too cold to wear the tiny suits my brothers and I wore, but just enough that we needed tuques, which just so happened to be somewhat colour coded. Blue for me, black for my middle brother and grey for the smallest of us. We were all ready for what seemed like a long trip, but in reality it was only five days of our time in the Big Apple. The wedding was on the second to last day of this voyage, and we were all excited as ever.

On the first day, we were making sure that the hotel room fit our standards, of which were coming from a small town, dwarfed in comparison to NYC, in the Great White North. What an adventure it was going to be. We checked under the beds for critters, we made sure the closet had enough space for five, we fluffed each pillow plenty of times to the point where they felt like big marshmallows. The place felt like home, to an extent. There was no television, the window looked almost directly into a brick wall, and the floorboards had a mighty creak when you planted your feet down. But, c'est la vie. We weren't there to be hotel room inspectors, we were there to see our uncle be the happiest man in the world for his own few moments before the title was taken from him by some other lucky fellow. By the time we were all settled in, the clocks said it was dinner time so off we went to a lovely Irish restaurant.

As our whole group of ten sat down, I could see the waitress let out a faint "Why do I still work here?" as she grabbed enough menus to cover up all the windows on the block, if required. As they landed on the table with a thud, she asked for drink orders noticeably unenthusiastically.

"What would you like to drink?" she asked, "Water, pop, juice..."

The list went on from there with various types of alcohol. As everyone ordered, I was browsing the menu for what I'd like for food rather than drink. When she came around to me, I forgot what I wanted, and nervously said nothing by accident. After our ordered food arrived, I asked quickly for a glass of water because after seeing the massive stack of chicken fingers I knew that I would need a drink to help me get through the whole meal. The same can be said about my youngest brother. He had ordered a burger so ridiculously huge that a picture was taken comparing it to the size of his five-year-old head.

After everyone finished their considerable meals, we took a walk around the neighborhood of the restaurant to see the attractions. Within five minutes of walking from the restaurant, you could make it to Grand Central Station, and a little farther you might find the Empire State Building. Once our self-guided tour was finished, we ended back up at the hotel we were booked in and turned in for the night. We needed our rest for the coming days, and decided to get a head start on it.

The next day we decided to take the same walk we did the day prior but this time in the light of day. It was very interesting to see the Empire State Building in the sunlight; it's height seemed so out of this world. Though the Empire State Building was very enchanting, it was not the only tall building we were going to see today. On our trip around town we found our way to Ground Zero. As I took in the sights and the emotion, I looked around at the people near, and they all seemed too bothered to stop for a second to think about the event and the aftermath. No, they were on their way to meet someone, late to a meeting, or just didn't want to. This seemed outlandish, as this tragedy had happened in this exact spot just ten years ago at the time. We then continued our journey to the centre of the apple, finding and seeing things I never thought to have, or could have existed. Namely a bowl-sized cone of ice cream that was comparable to my little brother's head again. Lots of big food in New York, eh?

From then on it was just more exploration of this vast concrete jungle. The preceding day we went to FAO Schwartz, an exciting adventure of toys and games built onto its own city block in NYC. As we entered the north entryway, I could see what I wanted to look at right away, the LEGO section. I'm not as fond of the construction toy now, but then it was the most enjoyable thing ever. Toys that allowed you to put your imagination to work? Really, man. It was the best. They had all kinds of sets and figures to choose from, even a wall that you could choose your own pieces, then build on your own to a fuller extent. As fun as it was though, there were two things wrong about that place: we were crunched for time, and there was an employee that almost seemed like he didn't like the word "fun." He would tell kids to quiet down, stop running and even to not play with the things left out for kids to try. He made the experience that much worse that I just wanted to leave, and so we did.

Later that night we went to my personal favourite restaurant, TGIFs. The building looked neat with it's unique decor, the food was incredible, and to top it all off, more big desserts. We sat and waited for what seemed like too long to my eleven-year-old hyperactive mind, but eventually we got our food. Once again, chicken fingers for me. We all told stories and personal experiences that we'd had on the trip so far, as we were, for the most part, split into smaller groups. Once the main course was done, here came the dessert. I had ordered a large piece of cake with some ice cream that looked smaller in the picture, as it was one of the featured items. It took one and a half people to finish that cake; I got a little help from my dad. Once we were done in that most wonderful restaurant, it was time to head to pseudo-home to get some rest for the next day of excitement.

The next day's task was to get familiar with the place where the marriage was to take place: Central Park. We had to take a taxi for this one. As we got into the magnificent golden carriage, here was a television on the back of each seat. Both were playing what I'm pretty sure was a *Saturday Night Live* skit featuring Jason Segel playing Andre the Giant ordering ice cream with silly names like "Moose Tracks" and "Tiger Stripe." I was so deeply interested in what he was going to order that I missed our cab driver scrape the side of an expensive looking SUV. What I didn't miss was the driver of said SUV let out a great "F*** YOU!" from the passenger window. Such a nice city, am I right?

When we arrived at the park, we found the fountain that our uncle was to be wed at the very next day. We scouted around to see if there was anything that would raise alarm at the wedding, and thankfully, there wasn't. Later that night we stopped by some candy stores near the hotel, and slept gleefully, knowing that the next day was the whole reason for that trip.

We woke up feeling great. Everyone was well-rested and we got our best clothes on, including our colour-coded tuques. First we had breakfast near the location of the wedding, then we went on a walk down the paths that led to that perfect spot. As we all stood around the husband and wife reciting their vows, I began to look around. Along the top of a bridge going over the paths we took, there were people starting to amass. As the ceremony concluded, there were more than triple the people up there than when I last looked. And when the married couple shared that ever so important kiss, the whole park, at least in our area, erupted. The cheers were so loud, I couldn't hear my dad asking me to line up for a picture. I was standing there still, smiling, and began to think over the whole trip. The bored waitress, the toy store employee, the angry SUV driver, even the people around Ground Zero. They didn't represent what I thought was an American or even a New Yorkian anymore. What I saw was people taking time out of their own day to make this occasion just that much more magical. I saw the good in people, and that rewrote whatever idea I had had about them before.

So, if you want to learn about the world, don't ask me. If you want to know about how wonderful travelling the globe is, don't ask me. If you want to know about anything but the immediate 100km around my house, don't ask me. But if you want to know about NYC and the people in it, then sure I could tell you. But don't take my word for it. Do me a favour and go, take a week-long trip there yourself. See the people, see the things that changed my view on the area outside of the comfort zone of my little North Bay

Chapter Seven

Living as a couple

Written by Gemma Dean

Was I worried about Matt and I living together after we had been living apart for two years? Definitely not. Was I worried about -50 weather and a lot of snow? Yes! After our fabulous wedding we journeyed back to Canada and headed far north to Iroquois Falls where Matt was renting a one bedroom flat close to St. Anne School where he was working. Well, it was cold and full of snow, but I was looking forward to going out and exploring some winter activities. It was quiet once Matt went back to work during the day, and I tried to keep myself busy by heading to the gym, going for a swim, even learning how to knit a bit. The weekends were always the best as we could spend our time together hanging out, heading to Timmins for our weekly shop, which meant hitting every shop to get the best deals as Matt sorted through the fliers earlier on in the week — oh how he loved a good bargain. There are several great memories of our time together in Iroquois Falls; the first was our mini moon at the Cedar Resort that Matt's colleagues and friends had organised as our wedding gift. It was in such a beautiful location where we spent the weekend relaxing and enjoying the spa. I did run out into the cold pool to swim a lap — shockingly cold! Wonderful food and company with the best man ever.

Matt took me one Saturday for my first cross-country skiing experience, which I was very excited about after dressing up in as many layers as I could to keep warm. We headed onto the cross-country trail, and it was quiet and beautiful as Matt played some music from our wedding as we skied. About halfway around we came to a mini hill, which we would go down. Feeling fairly confident on my skis now, I headed down first only to fall over sideways. I tried several times to get up and as a first-time skier it was not easy; the harder I tried, the more I fell back down, and those that know me well would know that I am now in floods of tears from laughter, which is only making it worse. Now you maybe wondering where my knight in shining armour is — well, he is filming the whole thing, with words of encouragement of course! I am sure around my twentieth attempt Matt decides I do need help or we may be here all day. Needless to say, I spent the rest of the time laughing as we skied.

Another memorable weekend with many winter firsts for me was a night we spent with Amber, Jan and their two lovely daughters, Amaya and Emerly, at their cottage outside of Iroquois Falls. Amber picked us up in her truck as we headed out into more snow-covered roads and forests. We needed to skidoo into the cottage, which would be my first Skidoo ride; I was very excited. On our way to the cottage the snow was getting fairly heavy and I am not sure what happened, but I do remember all of us falling off the Skidoo and, of course, I laughed really hard. Amaya and I watched on as Amber and Matt worked hard to dig it out from the snow. It took some time, but they managed it and we were back on our way. The rest of the afternoon was spent laughing, chatting, playing games and eating a good fish supper.

Sunday morning we woke early for a great breakfast and then some time out on the lake where I would get to drive a Skidoo. I knew I was doing a good job driving safely for the first time, only to be told by Matt I was driving like an old lady! There is video footage of this and it was pretty slow when I look back at it. Needless to say this was a great trip filled with many memories formed with lifelong friends.

In the middle of January, Matt and I journeyed down to Kingston to the international job fair to find a teaching position, as I was not a resident of Canada yet. We could not stay and we both wanted to see more of the world. We had several places in mind where we wanted to go, but Luxembourg and Malaysia were our top picks. It is a busy, crazy experience with all the different schools' presentations, interviews and decisions. On our second day we went to the Canadian International School (CIS) presentation where we met Glenn Odland who spoke about the school; both of us were immediately sold on CIS and Singapore. After interviewing with Glenn we had jobs outside the classroom though. I would be teaching swimming and Matt would be teaching drama, art and open minds. Not what we had in mind, but we were open to trying something new.

Chapter Eight

Honeymoon

Written by Gemma Dean

Where better than to head to Las Vegas for your honeymoon! Matt organised flights and hotel for the March break at the Venetian as we got engaged in Venice, Italy; he figured it was romantic. He also worked his magic to get us an upgrade on our room as it was our honeymoon. I had one job: to secure some shows while we were there. I booked us in to see *Love* by the Beatles Cirque du Soleil performance, which we were super excited to see, as well as a concert by Celine Dion. Unfortunately Celine was sick so the show was cancelled, so we rescheduled to see *Phantom of the Opera* with dinner.

For our first few days we strolled around all the different hotels checking them out, as well as heading down to the Vegas sign. If you go to Vegas head down to the sign — a guy was taking pictures and emailing them across to people for whatever you wanted to donate to him. We gave him $50 and got some great shots. Not sure if he is still there but worth a visit.

One of the scariest moments on our trip for me, was when we were in the New York section of a hotel heading for the roller coaster. We boarded the roller coaster and all of a sudden I had this sense of fear and needed to get off — I totally panicked — a side of me Matt had not seen before. Matt being the true husband who loves me so, gave some tough love and simply said to me, "Poops, know this — if we die, I love you." Needless to say it did not fill me with confidence. I spent the whole ride screaming my head off and after that we did not do anymore roller coasters! Looking back on it now it is funny and we did laugh about it a lot afterwards. I think more than anything I was embarrassed in front of all the other people that heard me screaming my head off.

Both of us were looking forward to the shows we had booked. Our seats were not great, but the show was not full so we asked to move to some balcony seats, which was not a problem once the show started. It was an amazing show and my first time experiencing a Cirque du Soleil performance; it would not be the last. The next day we were off for dinner and *Phantom of the Opera*, which I had been wanting to see for ages. I was wearing a really nice dress, which is kind of a rare deal but I thought I should impress as we were on our honeymoon and of course in "true Gemma fashion" spilt some of my dinner down me! So we had to go back to our room and change; luckily the show was in our hotel. Matt came to learn that I have a terrible habit of spelling food, particularly when I am wearing white. We had great seats for the show and it did not disappoint at all.

Nana and Papa (my grandparents) had given Matt and I some money for our wedding to use however we want. We made the decision while we were there to use this for a helicopter ride over the Grand Canyon and lunch on a ranch. Not being the biggest fan of heights, I braved the ride and it was so worth it. The views of the Grand Canyon are truly spectacular and we had front row seats in the helicopter, which meant we could see everything. I also got to hear the story of how Matt flew a helicopter during high school as part of a gifted programme — a story that I got to hear on more than just this occasion.

On our last day, we ended with a trip to the outlet malls. For those of you who knew Matt, you know that he loved to shop as well as find a good bargain. Myself on the other hand, not a massive fan of shopping, which Matt embraced. He always ensured I was well fed and watered before we started any kind of shopping. Many deals were had that day for both of us. We packed our new summer clothes to head back to freezing weather in Canada!

Chapter Nine

Moving to Singapore

Written by Gemma Dean

Well, our bags were all packed as we were jetted off for a new adventure together in Singapore. I was travelling from the UK as I had just completed a swimming course to work with my new role teaching swimming, and Matt was taking the long flight from Canada. I arrived first, Matt joined me at some ridiculously early hour of the morning. We were staying at a hotel downtown on Orchard Road, I totally don't remember the name of the hotel but it was really nice. The best thing that Matt enjoyed about the hotel was the breakfast — getting in his daily fix of bacon and chocolate croissants was most important. The week was super busy setting up new bank accounts, tours of the school (which seemed massive at the time) and finding an apartment.

During the week an agent named Jean picked us up with another couple from the school (Cody and Lizz) who we became good friends with during our time there. We spent most of the day touring around apartments close to school as that is what we had all requested, which was challenging as you are trying to make friends. When we came to our apartment I said to Matt you tell them we will take it before the other couple does! We all laughed about that in the years to come, but I didn't know them at the time and wanted that apartment, which was amazing and we spent the whole of our time living there. It had three bedrooms, living/dining room, kitchen and three bathrooms. Best of all, there was a swimming pool, gym and tennis courts. Now that I'm back in Canada, I remember how having a swimming pool where we lived really was the best. Change and head down to the pool, no need to gather your swimming things, get in the car and go somewhere; definitely miss that a lot. The area we were living in was also great. A twenty-minute walk to school or five minutes on the bike if you hit all the green lights. It became more like ten minutes as we took more of the scenic route whilst I was pregnant and the roads had become far busier. Five-minute walk to the MRT station (which is a train) that linked all around the island. We could take this to local shopping centres, which grew over the time we were living there. Best of all, a store started selling Costco products, which made Matt very happy, particularly after we had Carter as we could get reasonably-priced diapers and wipes.

We truly had the best time living and working in Singapore, and neither or us could have asked for a better time.

Chapter Ten

The Birth of Carter

Written by Gemma Dean

Matt and I knew we would like to have children at some point in our lives, however we wanted to spend some time together first as a couple, travelling around parts of Asia. So we did for the first few years that we were in Singapore, in addition to both of us enjoying different sporting activities. Matt was playing ice-hockey and floorball, and I became slightly hooked on triathlons. We joined an awesome club where we had fab coaches, and we made some lifelong friends and training buddies. After competing in several triathlons in Singapore, I plucked up the courage to do a half Ironman (1.9km swim, 90km bike ride and 21km run) in Tawian; it was great and I was hooked. So in 2015, I set my sights on completing a full Ironman before we were going to start a family. It was a tough year full of dedication and training, Matt was my rock of support through it all. That summer I completed Ironman UK (2.8km swim, 180km bike ride and a 42km run). It's such a big accomplishment that sometimes I wonder how I did it all.

After completing the Ironman, Matt and I were ready to start a family. Matt Googled to find the best doctor for us to see to make sure we were all good to start this journey. We found an Dr. Tan, an excellent doctor, and her staff were lovely as well. Both of us had tests done to make sure everything was all good to make babies. The news we received after the tests were done was not the best. She told me that I did not have many eggs and my uterus was not in the best shape it needed to be in. She said we may need to try IVF, but Matt told her not to worry that we would make babies, which Dr. Tan thought was absolutely hilarious. After several months we fell pregnant with Carter.

Carter was due to be born on December 21, and I was having a pretty good pregnancy. The last couple of months were definitely a struggle as I felt the size of an elephant and the heat in Singapore made everything very uncomfortable. Come the middle of November I started experiencing stomach cramps in the afternoon. By the end of the day it was bad, so I went to Matt's classroom only to find him not there and not answering his phone. After fifteen minutes of waiting he finally appeared to have me only burst into tears and tell him something was not right. Matt was ever the calming influence and we went off to get a taxi, down to the doctors. As soon as we arrived I was all hooked-up to check the baby. Well, I was having contractions so they admitted me into the hospital to keep an eye on me and gave me some medication to stop the contractions as we were six weeks early. I was also nervous as Dr. Tan was off to California to visit her daughter that day!! The on call doctor was very nice but not the same. With the contractions under control I was signed off work for a week and told to rest. Well, people who know me know that is easier said than done; I was bored out of my mind by the second day.

After our next checkup, the doctor said I could go back to work but was to take it easy. Well, we went back after a week and the contractions had started again, so that was it, signed off from work and back in the hospital on the December 6 for a C-section. Matt and I were so excited to meet Carter it all felt like a whirlwind. The staff at Mount Elizabeth Hospital were amazing — the best experience ever. Matt would say the best part was having a steak dinner every night! Carter was tiny and had jaundice so spent nearly the whole time under the lamp in the nursery. We only saw him when he needed feeding, which was super hard to do, as he was so sleepy all the time. It took Carter a while to get the whole breastfeeding thing down and we were lucky enough to have a great lactation consultant, as well as Matt being a super supportive husband who knew I would get there.

Four days later both Carter and I were given the all clear to go home from the hospital. It was a special moment bringing Carter home. The first night was by far the hardest, as he cried and cried. Neither Matt nor I could soothe him, so at about three in the morning Maya took over and peace came to the house. After that everything went so well as the three of us all pitched in shaping that first part of Carter's life.

Chapter Eleven

A Year Later

I was admitted to NUH for testing to find out the cause of the twitching. It was scary to say the least. Terrifying is more appropriate. They do not beat around the bush or sugar coat anything in Asia, which is either a blessing or a curse depending on how you look at it. I had a ton of blood work done. I had a CT scan, MRI and a spinal tap. This was the most uncomfortable experience with no pain. But nothing compares to the nerve tests where they stab you with a needle with a microphone in it so that they can listen to the behaviour of the muscles. Have you ever heard your muscles before? It is a strange sound somewhere between heartbeat and the sound of someone skipping to a heavy metal band.

I sat around most of the day watching show after show and the odd movie. It turns out that Gemma taught a son of one of the doctors who was treating me. He was surprised to see her at the hospital. I can't say enough good things about the way I was treated at the hospital. I want to thank Tyler for coming to visit me. It was greatly appreciated. The doctors had some theories as to what was wrong with me. It was either a nerve issue, an autoimmune disease or ALS. I knew what it was, but I didn't want to hear it. There was some debate over whether or not to go on our holiday to New Zealand or have a procedure known as a plasma exchange to see if it was an autoimmune disease. Guess what we did?

Chapter Twelve

Our Final Vacation to New Zealand

Written by Gavin and Clare Fuller

Matt had worked tirelessly (with persuasion, persistence, but also patience) on us for years and years to get us started on our international teaching adventure. In 2016, we set off to London to meet the head of the Canadian International School in Singapore with the hope that (as the head said) "The stars might align this year!" We had always hoped to get jobs in Singapore to be near Matt, Gemma and their growing family. Matt became part of our family and we part of his when we first met in Kochi, Japan, in 2001 (living side by side and taking in lots of trips together to explore the sights of Japan).

As so often happens in life, the stars didn't align again this time and Singapore didn't work out…but jobs in China did! We ended up living in a part of the world that was much closer to Singapore than England was. During our first year in China, we visited Matt and Gemma twice — first with Carter as a nicely cooking bump and second when Carter was a few months old. It was during these trips, amongst late nights watching *Last Man on Earth*, Chimichanga evenings and days exploring the sights of Singapore that the idea for our adventurous trip to New Zealand started to materialize…then the flights were booked and we were OFF for Christmas 2017/New Year's 2018!

By the time the New Zealand trip started, we all knew Matt's illness was becoming progressively more debilitating, and he was going through a terribly disempowering time. He was waiting for results from the US, but was already coming to terms with the worst. Confirmation would still take a couple of more weeks to arrive.

We started the NZ adventure separately; the Deans explored North Island and it was funny listening to Gemma talk about Frodo, *Lord of the Rings* land and the hundreds of photos she'd taken. We met up with the Deans in North Beach, Christchurch, Carter strapped safely to Matt and the Harrison bump growing nicely. Time with Matt and Gemma has always been special; there were always plenty of laughs, great food (and an assortment of ice cream or candy for Matt and Gav!). We both had some really honest conversations with Matt about his symptoms, the possible ALS diagnosis and choices he might choose to take in the future. But despite all this, it was incredibly hard to believe that this was happening to Matt. He had been our best buddy since we hung out in Japan all those years ago and has always had such a zest for life; his generosity and strength of commitment to family and friends has always been one of his outstanding attributes. It felt incomprehensibly unfair that this could be happening to Matt, Gemma, Carter and Harrison. Despite the clear signs that Matt was having difficulty with his balance and stamina, both he and Gemma kept everything as normal as possible for Carter and everything as calm as possible for growing Harrison. Matt also wanted the trip to be as normal as possible, taking part in everything that was going on.

We travelled about Christchurch a bit and had a road trip to Hanmer Springs, taking in a few beautiful wineries on the way (Pegasus Bay being a memorable one!). The usual combination of food, ice cream and some crazy golf at Hanmer Springs made the days fly by. We took on a boat trip from Akaroa, which was pretty bumpy. I shall never forget poor Gemma with her morning sickness on that boat; she literally filled up a whole bag but still had that beautiful, brave smile on her face.

Postscript:

There are many times people talk about what happens when we die. It seems too much to comprehend that we are no longer here. One of the things we have found to be true is the influence people have on each other's lives never disappears. The idea of six degrees of separation explains that we are never more than six social connections away from someone who knows us. This was brought starkly into light when we went to the Bangkok job fair in January this year. The fact that it was three years from the time we went to the London fair with the hope of landing a job in Singapore alongside Matt and Gemma was already very poignant when we arrived in Bangkok. When we got the message from Gemma on the first day of the fair, we knew in our hearts that Matt's condition had progressed to the point it had. We kept ourselves very busy on the first day of the fair, going to interviews and talking to lots of people.

At the very end of the first day, I (Gavin) stayed behind at the hotel the fair was being held in to finish a Skype interview with a school in Singapore. The job fairs are a crazy whirlwind of people and schools, some 650 candidates and 150 schools. When I went back into the candidates' lounge just after seven in the evening, there were only three or four candidates hanging around. I started talking to a young lady and asked how her first day was. She excitedly talked about some fantastic schools she was interested in; one of them in Senegal. It just happened to be the same school one of our closest friends in China is moving onto this summer when we finish. I told the young lady that she should mention my colleague in the second interview the next day. She asked how I was getting on and I explained that I had just finished a Skype interview for a school in Singapore. She mentioned that she was working in Singapore at the moment. When I asked which school, it came as no surprise, but hit me like a hammer, when she replied, "Canadian International." I choked up and mentioned Matt and Gemma. She knew all about Matt's condition and apologized. I managed to compose myself and talked about how we wouldn't have even been at the fair or started at an international school if it weren't for Matt. I explained that Matt wouldn't be alive for much longer and we talked for a bit about how unfair life can be. I went back to our hotel room to see Clare and we left our messages of goodbye for Matt.

Halfway through the next morning, I bumped into the same young lady on the stairs in between interviews and she burst into tears this time. She had just been for another interview at the school in Senegal, had mentioned me and my colleague from China, and had a really genuine talk with the head teacher. She then explained that she felt such a part of Matt's story, and as sad as we were, we talked about how lucky we felt to have been part of his life as well. We knew he would be happy that we had met and were talking on the other side of the world at a job fair in Bangkok.

We can never truly understand how much our actions and the things we do for others will impact and influence people's lives; it is an unfathomable thing. When Matt passed away, the tributes and stories that poured onto Matt's Facebook page gave some indication of how much he meant to people and the positive influence he had made. Matt will always be a part of us and we will always be better people for having been lucky enough to have known him as a true friend.

Chapter Thirteen

The Beginning of the End

So when we returned from New Zealand, I was straight back in the hospital for a plasma exchange and more blood tests, lung tests, X-rays, more nerve tests and a muscle biopsy. I was such a rare case that they kept my blood and muscle to study.

So a plasma exchange? What is it? Just like what it sounds like. You have to have a bunch of tubes put in your neck and then they hook you to a machine that swaps out your old plasma for new plasma. I almost died during the first exchange but they had a team of doctors arrive in time. I don't know how serious it really was but it went from two nurses to doctors plus more nurses. I turned out to be okay and did two more exchanges with no problem.

The last test was a muscle biopsy. It was not painful but strange. You could hear all the noise associated with slicing and dicing meat. Then I had six weeks of treatment to suppress my immune system and hopefully reboot it. But that didn't work. My nerve tests showed degradation in nerve response time since my last test, but the smoking gun was the muscle biopsy. It showed what I feared most, wastage.

Chapter Fourteen

Matt's Diagnosis

Written by Gemma Dean

When I saw this section I knew it would be hard to write about how I felt. There are certain words which come to mind when we were first told this news: shock, devastation, holy shit, WTF, you must be wrong this can't be happening to Matt, to us! When Matt first went to get some testing done in October because his muscles were continuously twitching and he came to tell me what the possibilities could be, I just couldn't believe it. I was definitely in shock. None of these outcomes sounded great, so they really must have been wrong. The next month or so was like torture for both of us having more testing done and waiting.

After having multiple blood tests, muscle biopsies, MRIs, CT scans — you name it, Matt had it — they decided to do a plasma exchange. This took place after the Christmas holidays, as we wanted to visit New Zealand in our break because we were not sure if this would be our last holiday as a family. I do not even remember the time frame after the plasma exchange, maybe a week, when we went back to the doctor's to get the results. We were both hoping and praying for some good news, but I think we both knew that it was not good. The thought of Matt having ALS was terrifying, as there was no time frame on how long he had, what was going to happen and when it would happen. We both knew so little about this disease, only what we had Googled, and none of that had a miracle ending.

Once we were in the doctor's office and he told us the official diagnosis was ALS, I sat there and I honestly could not believe what he was saying. Multiple questions and thoughts raced through my head, and I could not even begin to imagine what Matt was thinking. This news was truly soul- and earth-crushing. How could I be losing my best friend, lover, husband, soulmate, father to my kids, my everything.

As we prepared to move home, I was half expecting the hospital to call us and apologise for making a huge mistake with Matt's diagnosis, or that I was going to wake up for this horrible nightmare I had been in. Unfortunately that never happened. Over the coming months I would watch the person who I love, change and deteriorate from this awful, unyielding, unforgiving disease that shows no sign of hope. Nothing ever changed the way I loved and felt about Matt throughout this whole ordeal and never will. He will always be the best part of my life.

Life can be truly cruel in the worst possible ways.

Chapter Fifteen

Our Return to Canada

Written by Gemma Dean

We made the decision after Matt's diagnosis to move back to Canada so that we would be closer to his family. It was not the way we wanted or imagined it would be moving back to Canada. We had hoped that Matt would get a job at an IB school and that I would stay at home with the boys for a couple of years. A very different scenario now presented itself to us. That being said, CIS was great booking us business class tickets back to Canada with a quick stop off in the UK to see some of my family. In addition to our landlady not charging us anything, allowing Maya (our nanny) to stay there, as well us leaving behind all the furniture, which made all of that slightly easier for us to get things sorted.

My biggest concern was flying at thirty-five weeks pregnant!! I got the all clear from Dr. Tan who I was truly sad would not be delivering Harrison. I know Matt was looking forward to more steak dinners at Mount Elizabeth's. I don't think they have this service in many other countries. We found an airline I could fly on, so not a problem, just had to keep my legs crossed and hope that a baby did not pop on the plane. He did not pop out until the 27th of April, thank goodness.

We packed all our bags, got in a large taxi with Matt's cousins who were visiting (Erica, Pat and Ayden), along with our good friend, Scott, who drove some of our luggage in his car. We met our friends, Vera and Jan, at the airport for a quick goodbye as well. It was an emotional goodbye to our friends, colleagues, training buddies and to a country we truly loved being a part of for six years. If you ever get a chance to visit this amazing city make sure you do.

The flight over to the UK was a long one — thirteen hours with a fifteen-month-old who only wanted to sit on mummy's very pregnant belly, which meant plenty of trips to the bathroom. Once we arrived in London, we waited for Alyssa (Matt's sister) to join us as she was going to fly back to Canada with us to help out with Carter and all of our stuff, which there was a fair bit of.

After a couple days in the UK visiting with family, we took the slightly shorter flight to Canada where I have to say Carter was awesome and pretty much slept the whole way. After a night in the hotel airport we were picked up by Andrew and Josh (Matt's brothers) to make our way back to North Bay. We stayed there with Betty whilst organising ourselves for the arrival of Harrison, as well as sorting out other bits and pieces and getting some renovations done on the cottage so we could move in during the summer.

ศูนย์อุตสาหกรรมทำร่ม
UMBRELLA MAKING CENTRE

83

WELCOME
TO Fabulous
LAS VEGAS
NEVADA

Chapter Sixteen

The birth of Harrison

Written by Gemma Dean

Carter was around seven months old and it was the summer holidays when I started to feel broody again. Matt and I discussed having another baby, which we both really wanted so that was an easy decision to be made. There was a timeline though: Matt said we only had until October to get pregnant, as that was when my Bupa (private medical care) would run out. Come the end of August we were pregnant with baby number two; it took us both by surprise that it had happened so quickly. This one seemed a lot harder to keep a secret, and most people found out around seven weeks as I just couldn't hold the excitement in any longer.

We made an appointment with Dr. Tan — we were super happy to have her again. She confirmed we were pregnant and a few months later we found out that we were having another boy. Next step was the great name hunt. We found it hard enough to decide on Carter. I started by putting all the names forward I really liked and, obviously, Matt did not like any of them. His were no better. We were watching Indiana Jones and the Last Crusade one night and I said how about Harrison (after Harrison Ford) and that was what we settled upon. Harrison it was, Harry for short.

As Harry grew over the next few months, our lives changed forever with Matt's diagnosis of ALS and our decision to move back to Canada at thirty-five weeks pregnant. Andrew and Andrea managed to get us in with their doctor, Dr. Waja, and we were both super-pleased to have a doctor to go back to in Canada. Once we met him and his super-lovely team we both became very relaxed about having the baby. The next few weeks went by as a bit of a blur as we began sorting our stuff out at Betty's, preparing for the arrival of a baby, getting a new car, obtaining health cards and getting things organised for Matt so we could make everything as easy as it could be under the circumstances.

On the April 27, I was booked in for a C-section at 8:30 in the morning. We arrived early in the morning. I cannot even remember the time, but Alyssa, who would be staying with me overnight so Matt could rest as much as possible, drove me there. The nursing team was great at the hospital, but we did miss the food from Mount Elizabeth. Alyssa got us some pizza the first night after Harrison was born. We were super-lucky to have both Matt and Alyssa come into the room after the C-section. Matt was too worried about holding Harry just in case something happened.

Harry was a lovely little bundle of joy who spent more time with me than Carter did right after birth, which was a lovely experience. He spent some time in the NICU as his sugars were so low but was out after a while. He went onto formula as well as he wasn't feeding properly. You would think the second time around would be easier — apparently not. Matt was still as supportive as ever and knew I could do it. Three days later we were discharged to go home and start life as a family of four with an expected twist thrown in.

Chapter Seventeen

A Trip to Halifax

Written by Andrew Dean

Before every trip I sent an email to the manager of the hotel which looked something like this!:

> Dear Scott,
>
> My name is Matt Dean and I have ALS. My little brother and I are coming to Halifax as a bucket list trip before I die. We plan on going to Oak Island and touring the outlying areas as well as the city. I have booked a room with two queen size beds. Is it possible to have a room with two queen size beds with a disabled washroom? This trip is to show my appreciation to my little brother for helping me throughout all of this ordeal. We plan on doing as much as possible while we are there as long as I can manage.
>
> I guess what I am asking is for a few small favours. We need to know the best places to get a burger and steak in the city. I would also like to request the materials necessary to build a kick-ass fort and stock it with some of his favourite snacks: dill pickles, dill pickle chips, ketchup chips, Reese's Peanut Butter Cups, and anything you feel that is tasty from

the Halifax area that we might not know about because we are from Ontario.

Thank you for your help,

Matt

Preface:

Roughly four years ago, Matt calls me from the other side of world (not sure which country this time — haha) and says to me, "Hey, have you watched *The Curse of Oak Island* on History?"

"No."

Matt encouraged me to watch it. After I ignored Matt's MANY attempts, I promised him I would watch two episodes and see where it went. I thought a show about a curse would be silly and, frankly, that is all I knew about the show or Oak Island. Matt had taught about Oak Island while teaching in the Middle East and Russia. He used the old CBC archives' videos, articles, YouTube clips, etc. to create interest for his students about history, treasure hunting, research, and curses.

I believe Andrea and Mackenzie were away and I finished the first season of the show over the course of a weekend, not just the two episodes I had promised. I was hooked. Matt and I were now discussing everything Oak Island! We discussed many movies, shows, sporting events over the phone across the world from one another, late at night, or the wee hours of the morning while our loved ones often slept. It was "our" time to talk. Our talks were about kids, our jobs, our lives…but it always, and I mean always, ended up about Oak Island.

Mother's Day 2018

Matt and his family have returned home from Singapore, we know the diagnoses, we know the outcome. We are sitting in our mother's backyard on Mother's Day discussing things that Matt wanted to accomplish while he could. He said he wanted to do something with each of his siblings. All of us being adventurous in our own right started throwing out ideas. Matt turned his head and looked at me, "Oak Island?" and without hesitation I said "Yep." I should have known better; I should have replied, "Let's look into it," or "Might be an option, Matt." If you knew Matt, the other responses would have bought me some time to wrap my head around it. That night, I was getting emailed potential dates, flight times, hotels, what else we could do or see while in Halifax, etc. Matt never hesitated when it came to adventure, and he was all-in for Oak Island; so was I.

Within two days, we had a date, flights booked, hotels booked and no idea if we could even get close to Oak Island. I guess that was the adventure, or the reality of knowing this was it — this was living the little life he had left.

From here on out, I won't discuss Matt's condition, but let's say the obvious signs of his disease were setting in and were noticeable to anyone who came in contact with Matt.

Day 1

May 19, 2018 (yes, that fast. Mother's Day was the 13 — haha!).

Off to Ottawa to catch a flight in the morning of the twentieth to Halifax. We had just passed Bonfield, Ontario, and were not yet in Mattawa (for those not from around here, it's roughly 25-30 minutes outside of town). Pouring rain, wipers full speed, car full speed, red flashing lights behind us full speed — haha! Yep, pulled over. And because my mom will read this, I was only doing 15 over. The cop was not happy about the rain coming down and getting out of his car, so we started our trip with a speeding ticket. I'm telling you this next part because if you knew Matt and our relationship (likely the same with so many of you), you would understand. After accepting the ticket, rolling up my window and placing my driver's licence back in my wallet, I looked at Matt and said, "You couldn't play your 'dying' card for me, eh?"

Matt, stoned faced: "I tried, but the ALS wouldn't let me speak!"

I couldn't pull away, we were laughing so hard we had tears in our eyes. Not even an hour out of town and already making memories.

Later that day, and I mean later than our agreed upon time for arrival because Matt (and again, if you know him) had to stop at Tangler Outlet Mall to look for deals. We arrived at the Chateau Laurier right around dinner time. We decided to head down to the market, grab a bite and do some sight seeing. We had dinner at the fifties diner, complete with milkshakes and all. After dinner, we cruised the market until we found a small shop that was making homemade, fresh donuts. Yep, grabbed some of those for the walk back to the hotel.

After a long day, it was time for some rest and the airport in the morning. Not before a knock at the door — a lovely cheese and fruit tray had been sent to our room by the manager of the Chateau. It was lovely, and the time spent with my brother eating food in bed and watching playoff hockey reminded me of when we were kids.

Day 2 - Halifax

We arrived in the afternoon and picked up our baby blue four-door jeep; it was that or some other crap SUV/little car. I stand by our decision to draw attention to ourselves — haha! We drove into downtown Halifax and searched out our hotel. We climbed the steep hills and eventually arrived at our destination. The Prince George Hotel! I can't say enough great things about this hotel, what they did, or the memories they helped create. When Matt booked the room, he had asked for a handicapped room. The manager contacted Matt through his email (and no one would want this job) asking Matt how severely he was handicapped because their handicapped rooms were double-booked by accident. Matt explained where he was in his journey and that he had me for help. The most important things were walk-in shower and accessible toilet. The manager explained they had a nice room that wasn't "handicapable" but would likely handle his needs. In an effort to offer amazing customer service, the manager emailed Matt back asking what he could do to make it up to him. Matt being Matt replied that we like to eat bad food, build kick-ass forts and go for burgers.

When we got into our room, Matt and I were speechless! (hard for both of us — haha!). The hotel manager and staff went above and beyond. They had a table set up with bags of chips, apple juice, chocolates, mints, ginger beer, nuts, pickles, all local products. Complete with a map to the best burger restaurants in town as voted on by the staff. If that wasn't enough, we turned the corner where there were two wooden signs that read "The Deans'" "Kick ass Fort." There was a giant box of plastic plumbing corners, elbows and many, many feet of plastic pipe and extra blankets and sheets to build our very own fort. This was the coolest! I can't explain the giddiness of two grown men, laughing, crying and building a kick-ass fort in our hotel room. We cracked our ginger beers and got to work. We built our fort…but it wasn't complete. More on this later.

After building our fort, we were hungry, but Matt didn't feel like a burger yet, so we agreed on The Cut Steakhouse. We had a candle-lit dinner (haha!) with sixty-day, dry-aged steaks, complete with Caesars, baked potatoes, carrots and crème brûlée for dessert. It was an amazing meal and a great dinner with my big brother. Likely a little too romantic for brothers, but the ambiance and quiet was welcomed considering the levity of the situation.

After dinner, we walked the boardwalk until Matt decided he was tired and needed to "pimp" our fort — haha, yes you read that right. We drove to a Dollarama (another Matt staple), grabbed a bunch of string lights — different kinds in case there was a design change — and batteries to run them. We headed back to the hotel, "pimped" our fort and took turns taking pictures with what we created. It was like we had built the pyramids or painted the Sistine Chapel — our chests were inflated with how proud we were — haha!

At this point, it was roughly 8-9pm and Matt got a second wind. He wasn't ready to go to bed so early while in Halifax. He stated that healthy Matt would kick sick Matt's ass for going to bed early, so we put our shoes on and headed back out. We headed for the Casino to lose some money. We walked around, placed a few bets here and there until Matt found his machine — he said it spoke to him. I wish this story ended with excitement and we pulled the one armed bandit for a couple thousand, but truth be told Matt and I each put in $20 and pulled for ZERO! But we were happy, it was time together.

It was then back to the hotel for bed!

Day 3 - OAK ISLAND!!!

We both woke early, as we were beyond excited about venturing to Oak Island. We started the roughly 45-50 minute drive to Oak Island we enjoyed the sunshine, the drive, the scenery and the excitement in our stomachs about the journey we were taking on a whim, on a last-minute idea, on a dying man's wish. We had tried reaching out to Oak Island, Prometheus Entertainment, cast members, etc., etc., etc. to no avail, but that was OK, we were going anyways.

We arrived at the Island to find a sandwich-board at the beginning of the causeway saying the island was closed but the interpretive centre would be open later in the day. A little bummed out, we headed back a few kms to a hotel we had passed called The Atlantica (it is now called the Oak Island Resort). We pulled in and went for breakfast to kill some time. It was a lovely buffet breakfast overlooking the bay and all the islands you could handle (what a view). We finished up, both of us still excited, and headed back to the island. This time the sandwich-board said the interpretive centre was open. We took pictures and video of our excitement, but that's for me and Matt's two boys when they are ready.

We crossed the causeway...We arrived...OAK ISLAND!

There is a parking lot, the interpretive centre, the war room and then a large security gate, trailers, vehicles and lots of people working in an area you won't get to (more on this later). There is also a house that is visible from the parking lot and that was Dan Blankenship's home, who recently passed. On a 140-acre island, you are talking four or five acres of access (estimating). That didn't bother us one bit. We were there, we were happy, we were together.

We took some photos of the memorial for those who have passed trying to find the treasure and then headed over to the war room, which seemed to be locked up and kind of sitting in the open, not as we had pictured it from the show. We also peeked in the windows and it was full of stuff, like a shed would be. This confused both Matt and I. Were they not shooting the show anymore? Did they have another war room and this was a replica? More on this later…

We headed into the interpretive centre! It's a museum, a tribute, a time capsule of the people that have come before the Laginas and the efforts they have made with their team. It's a wonderful walk through the history of the island complete with the *Reader's Digest* article, artifacts that have been found, countless maps and ideas on where the treasure might be. This space is warm, welcoming and sure to excite everyone who walks through the doors, whether you are six years old or ninety. It's truly magical to see the work that has been accomplished over 200 years of searching this island.

We spent a couple hours reading everything they had posted, and of course hit the souvenir section, which will lead us into what happened and how it impacted our lives forever. I don't say that lightly — it truly impacted us and will be with me for the rest of my life. I can't wait to share the stories with Matt's boys.

While in the shop, we picked up stuff for everyone we could think of — couldn't leave anyone out on our journey to Oak Island. However, there was one thing that was calling my name. It was a hand-drawn, artistically-created map of Oak Island by a local artist. It was beautiful, and it was something I had to have. It was my piece of the island I would bring home as my keepsake of the time I travelled to Oak Island with my big brother. Little did we know, it was a starting point of what was to come.

After cashing out, my new-found map in hand, Matt and I headed back outside. I turned right to head to the Jeep, Matt turned left to head to the large gate and signs that said no trespassing, filming in progress, etc.

I said, "Matt, what are you doing?"

He said, "Just taking a look."

I hurried back in his direction, map in hand. We hung around the gate for a few minutes and Matt being Matt, he was trying to figure a way around the gate. No seriously, he was. I guess part of us was hoping to see one of the cast members or catch a glimpse of the crew that filmed the show. Out of nowhere, this little Fiat car came over the hill from the other side of the gate...the gate opened. We stood off to the side and the car went past, but pulled into a spot not far from where we had been standing. A woman stepped out of the car and asked if she could help us.

This is where it all began...

Matt and I wandered over closer to the woman. We introduced ourselves, her name was Karlie. I truly believe Karlie was sent to us. We chatted her up, I explained who, what, when and why we were there. As fate would have it, Karlie had a personal friend fighting the same fight as Matt was. She asked if we could hang tight for a minute while she went over to handle something at one of the production trailers. When she came back, she asked if we wanted to stick around for a bit and she would introduce us to Rick on his lunch break. She also stated that there was a good chance she could get him to autograph my map. Needless to say, Matt and I were very giddy and quite emotional. Tears were shed, excitement grew; this was more than we could have ever imagined. Getting to meet the star of the show and the driving force behind what was being done on the island was amazing.

Lunch time came, SUVs, side-by-side, four wheelers, all started pulling into the production trailers. It was the cast and crew breaking for lunch. Matt and I were sitting under a tree out of the sun right beside the gate. Karlie came out to us and said Rick will be right down for a meet and greet. You couldn't wipe the smile from our faces. Out of nowhere, Rick appears and he is headed our way wearing his Dr. Pepper T-shirt, signature blue jeans and carrying his signature blue jean long sleeve button up. He is a tall man, quiet, honest, authentic, genuine and truly caring. He extended his hand to Matt, Matt broke down. His hand couldn't grip the way I'm sure he wanted to and he couldn't speak the words I know he wanted to say. I intervened and explained to Rick what was happening, and as Matt calmed his emotions, he would be able to communicate more effectively. Rick and I began a dialogue until Matt was able to speak. After a couple of minutes, Matt and I began to share our story with Rick, about watching the show a world apart and how Matt taught the story of Oak Island in various countries. Really, truthfully, we couldn't have met a nicer man. We kept telling him to go, have lunch, you have work to do and he continued to hang out and chat with us. He then asked me about the map that he too was fond of. We asked if he would sign, he said, "Of course, but let me go see if Charles (Barkhouse) is around to sign it too." AWESOME!! Another cast member signature, how cool is that? Rick was gone for a few minutes and as he made his way back, he brought Charles Barkhouse. Shit just got real!! Haha! Another amazing, highly intelligent, genuine man. He expressed to Matt right away his deepest sympathies of his diagnosis and began discussing the island with us right away. He was very curious to hear our thoughts and ideas about the island, the treasure, the who, what, when, why in our heads. It couldn't have been a better 45 minutes to hour. It was a blessing and very touching; they gave up their lunch hour to spend time with us. Rick even brought plates of food over to us to eat with him.

Matt and I could see the crew behind Rick and Charles starting to head back out. We knew our time with these fine gentlemen had come to end. So, we thought. Rick stepped away and spoke with Karlie. Upon his return, Rick explained they had some work to do this afternoon, but asked us if we wanted to come back around 4:30 p.m. and have a little look at the island. WOW! As stated above, shit just got real. We were both emotional and couldn't hide it. Rick knew: two brothers on an adventure and this was way, way beyond our expectations. We happily accepted and went into Mahone Bay and then onto Lunenburg to kill some time and return to the island at 4:30 p.m. All other plans or ideas were on hold.

Matt and I hit up the flower shop and liquor store to purchase thank you gifts for Rick, Charles, Karlie and Dave Blankenship whom we had seen in the distance when talking with Rick. We arrived back at the island at 4:30 p.m., and Rick and Charles were waiting for us. They had a side-by-side ready for us. For the next three hours, they (joined by Dave throughout as well) gave us our own personal tour of the island. They showed us everything — and I mean everything; 10X, Money Pit, Nolan's Cross, Nolan's property, the swamp, the new war room, H-8, Smith's Cove, Cave-In Pit, etc., etc., etc. EVERYTHING! Charles gave us the most in-depth history lesson of our lives. We asked questions, told stories, laughed, cried and truly had the experience of a lifetime. Rick took us to his "special spot" on the island. It's a spot he goes to reflect. It's a great spot and few people know where it is. It was an honour he took us there and shared his spot with us.

When returning to the gate that goes to the parking lot, Karlie was waiting with Joe. There was a group of men — producers, directors, camera men, etc. (I truthfully can't remember everyone's name and title because Matt and I just had the greatest experience of our lives together, we were on a natural high) — who stuck around to meet us and ask if we had plans for tomorrow.

"No, no plans—" haha!

They asked us if we wanted to come back in the morning and spend the day with the team and watch how they film for the show, etc. Shit just got real!! Never in our wildest dreams could we have dreamt something like this up. This show is the number 1 show in the world. Watched all over the world and Matt and I spent years of our lives watching, reading and debating one another about. We were gobsmacked and of course accepted their invitation.

We headed back to the hotel, calling our wives and our mother to share the news on what had just transpired. After sharing our adventure with everyone, it was time to go to bed. It was a long day for Matt, but he was a trooper and didn't let ALS slow him down.

In the morning, we woke up with a spring in our step, headed downstairs for breakfast at the Prince George (fantastic) and then began our journey to Oak Island.

We arrived at Oak Island early, bringing Tim Horton's doughnuts for the crew. Ready to see how this day will unfold, we sat quietly watching the team get ready for their day. At this point a producer's assistant came over to Matt and I and asked us to sign an NDA. Of course we did and as they say, the rest is history. What happened that day on the island is only known between the cast and crew, Matt and myself. And it will forever stay that way. Sempre Avanti.

Chapter Eighteen

A Trip out West

Written by Alyssa Dean

Matt has always been a world traveller. My first three nephews lovingly refer to him as "Uncle Travelling Matt." The stories, as you've read so far, inspire wanderlust, so my goal is to come close to that feeling in weaving the tale of our time together out west this summer.

When Matt and Andrew returned from their whirlwind tour of Oak Island and the east coast, the travel bug bit Matt once again mid June. I came home from work one day to Matt cruising airline websites and various iterations of Expedia. He was bound and determined to see the mountains one more time. I admire that about him: once he gets an idea in his mind, there's no stopping his efforts or his enthusiasm. On June 12, Matt sent me the itinerary he crafted on Expedia: Vancouver, Whistler, Squamish, Calgary, Banff, Canmore. The hotels? Hilton Whistler Resort & Spa, Fairmont Vancouver Airport, Banff Caribou Lodge & Spa, and Sheraton Suites Calgary Eau Claire. Like I said... there is no stopping his efforts or his enthusiasm. So, on Sunday, June 24, we set off to Toronto to crash in a dive hotel (neither of us will ever forget the lady of the evening I saw in the parking lot while I packed up the car a few days later) before our flight home. I say "dive" because of the earwigs and shady looking sheets, not the prostitute — she's just gotta pay her bills like everyone else. And, to be fair, we were in her house. Anyway.

The flight out to British Columbia was smooth. We grabbed breakfast at the hotel before leaving for the flight, so when we boarded and saw that we were going to have "second breakfast," I was pumped. Matt didn't get my "second breakfast" joke, so I publicly disowned him on social media. Regardless, we chowed down on pancakes, maple butter, chicken sausage and cran-apple compote with fresh fruit and yogurt.

We landed in Vancouver, and it felt like going home. The totems in the airport terminal reminded me of when I flew to BC for the first time in 2006. My crazy brother had convinced his outdoor adventure camp to take on his little sister as a counsellor — but I'll get to that a little later. When we went to find our car rental place, we walked out the same doors where I was picked up twelve years previously. We took the shuttle to the car rental, and our trusty Dodge Caravan was prepped, chipped windshield and all. With that, we set off for Whistler.

Driving down the Sea to Sky is breathtaking even when it's raining, which it usually is. We pulled off into Squamish on the way to Whistler because being there once in our trip just wasn't enough. We went to the old lot where Camp Summit used to live and found a giant house, so, of course, we crept down the driveway to take a peek. Casual stalking. Nothing serious. I tried to convince Matt that we had to eat at the Watershed Grill because we spent so much time there as counsellors. Fries were cheap and Lord knows we weren't making any money at that gig (but that wasn't the point, was it?). Instead, we stopped in Brackendale to eat at the Crabapple Cafe because Sunrise Sushi in Squamish was also no longer a thing. I had curry and Matt had a veggie crap (okay "crap" was a full-on autocorrect, but I'm sticking with it) and fries (I seriously can't believe that was his first big meal out on our trip!).

Once our bellies were full, we headed off to Whistler. It was raining, so the main part of Whistler, the Village, was pretty quiet. We puttered around and looked to see what sort of trouble we could get into the next day when the sun promised to make an appearance (ish). Ultimately, we decided on going up the Peak 2 Peak Gondola. The next day, we travelled up Blackcomb and Matt told me stories about his kids from Summit; he had taken the kids up the trails to get eaten by bears... I mean, for a hike. We made it to the top and it was freezing, but we were pretty pleased with the ride. We searched for bears the entire time — once a mountain counsellor, always a mountain counsellor. The best part of choosing the Peak 2 Peak wasn't the bear hunt, the spectacular views or the fresh air...we cut the very, very long line because of Matt's wheelchair...there may or may not be photographic evidence of us giving a thumbs-up once we were seated and heading up the mountain. Matt's grin may or may not be completely devilish in said photos. You'll never know, though.

Once we came down the mountain, we packed up the van and headed back toward Squamish. Whistler had been swell, but we had places to go and people to see in the little town that once employed us. Our original plan was to see the new Camp Summit site and to visit with Parky, Daphne and the girls for as long as we could until we had to make the trek back to Van. We arranged to see Summit and the Parks in the late afternoon on the 26. So our morning and early afternoon in Squamish saw us cruising our old haunts. In particular, we stopped at what was the Sunflower Cafe for lunch and, more importantly, gelato. Matt's cone shadowed nearly half his face when he held it up (by the way, that's how you know you're doing gelato right). Matt also dragged me to a dollar store...because Matt.

But, before long it was time to hit up Summit. It was a long haul out to the new site — comparatively speaking, that is. The old site was right in town, though it rarely felt that way. The new site sits N 49°53.532 and W 123°15.438, deep into the Squamish Valley. Parky and family live on the site, and their home is beautiful — a reflection of the people inside. In classic Parky style, he rode up on the golf cart and gave us both big bear hugs. He wanted to show us the entire site via golf cart, so off we went. (It should be noted that I stood/hung on to the side of the cart for dear life...it really is a two-seater. What were we thinking?) The site had many of the structures from the original site, which is a testament to Parky and the staff's efforts to be environmentally friendly and sustainable. It was incredible to see it in person because it's clear we missed it and the people it comes with. After we puttered around and enjoyed reminiscing with Parky, we drove up to the staff house so Parky could show Matt that he still had his Summit ring (this is a Matt thing…he always makes stuff that represents the places he's been and their impact on his life). When we entered the staff lodge, there were pictures hung everywhere of former staff holding the Summit flag in the most amazing places all over the world. Low and behold, there was Matt holding up the flag…in Czech? Who knows. He's been so many places, it's tough to keep up! We also managed to find the plaque that showed Matt's team winning the camp Olympics. I'm fairly certain I have a picture of Matt in his "I'm kind of a big deal" pose with it.

Summit shows how deeply people can impact a space. I love that Matt will live on on that wall for every camper and staffer to see as they make their own Summit memories. We had a tear-filled goodbye with Parky, D and the girls. He helped Matt into the car with strength, but what Matt doesn't know is after Parky closed the van door, he came to me, put his arms around me, and just collapsed. He balled. All 6'6" of him was feeling the goodbye deeply. I will never forget that hug — he meant it with everything he had. Seeing Summit in the rearview as we drove away reminded me of this whole situation we're in: there are times when you look back and cry because what you see is what you had — everyone decides for themselves whether those are tears of misery or tears of joy.

Back in Vancouver we returned the Caravan — oh so sad. Not! (That is a solid *Wayne's World* reference) — and headed to the Fairmont. We walked into our hotel room and we were full-on blown away by the effort they put into our stay (though not surprised because Matt is a big deal and he let them know he was coming). In our room, they built us a castle out of cardboard that housed all of Matt's favourite types of candies. On the table were Matt's favourite chips and Perrier water. But, the highlight? They had set up a faux tent with all one might need to camp overnight. What might that be? Well, a lantern, some pillows, and costumes to dress up in, of course. Impressive, right? There's more. In the bathroom, they had personalized the shampoo, conditioner, hand cream and body wash. That's right…they all had "Mr. Matthew J. Dean" written on them (remember: he's kind of a big deal…). The detail was so small but so significant, and that's how I'll always choose to remember this trip. We did such small things, but each of them was significant to Matt, and I'll never forget the moments each of those small things turned into the big things for him.

We landed in Calgary around noon on the 27. Matt's buddy, Odie, was there to take us to lunch and to pick up our rental. This time we got a Santa Fe (peace out Caravan-driving-soccer-mom-version-of-me). Seeing Matt and Odie hug in the terminal broke my heart, but also somehow filled it with a tremendous amount of joy. You see, the whole trip was like this. A "goodbye tour," if you will. People hugged him like they knew it was their last hug, that each one counted more than all their past hugs put together. Matt and Odie's hug was special because you could tell they meant something to one another.

Odie was also the kind of friend that took the time to put together three sweet surprises for Matt. It started with a basket of snacks and entertainment for our trip to Banff. Cherry Pepsi (because Coke isn't as common out west, I guess), chips, chocolate, beer…and a Tragically Hip CD. Did I mention that Matt was wearing his "In Gord We Trust" T-shirt that day? Kismet. We went to some Irish pub a short drive from the airport. We sat down and Odie offered up his second sweet surprise of the day: a 44-second video clip of Kelly Hrudey. He spoke of Matt's passion for helping kids and his efforts at camp, but he also took the opportunity to tell Matt that there's still something about Matt that bugs him... that he scored on Kelly in a shinny game. Legend has it that the shinny winners were given a handmade Stanley Cup. So, wouldn't you know it, Odie's third and final surprise was a replica of that faux shinny Stanley Cup. It was incredible. We laughed and cried about this tinfoil-wrapped thing. Odie owned the goodbye tour at this point. It was so clear how much he loves Matt. I hope we meet again one day so that I can tell him how special those moments were and how valuable it was to see Matt smile when they happened.

Cherry Pepsi and Heineken in hand (not literally…one of us had to drive our asses to Banff), we made our way to our next destination: Banff Caribou Lodge & Spa. Matt met a few friends there in the lobby, and then we met up with his friend, Darrin, for dinner at the Keg. Steak and crème brûlée, that's what Deans do. Matt and Darrin told story after story, but in particular, discussed the local legion as a haunt from their day — these guys were old when they were young, I tell ya. So, when Darrin suggested he take Matt out to get up to some shenanigans, I couldn't say no. I mean…how much trouble could they get into if they were just going to see that same legion? To this day, I don't know exactly what they got up to, but I trust that it was shenanigans because Matt came back tired and happy. It's all I could ask for.

The next morning, we slowly made our way to breakfast with Darrin before seeing him off back home. After, we cruised around Banff checking out shops. No trip with Matt is solid without visiting as many knick-knack stores available, which sounds like a mean sibling comment but, the truth is, it's because he's so thoughtful. He's always looking for a small token of his experience to bring home and share with everyone, and he's always (literally every. single. time) finding little treasures for you too. They're all over my house. Every time I cook, I see the spoon rest from Whistler and it brings me back. Like I said before, something so small becomes so significant.

KANANASKIS TOMORRROOOWWWWWWW. I REALLY LOVE YOU, MATT.

I wrote that statement above because in classic Matt Dean fashion, I had to write this book with him over the days leading up to January 11. He'd write at night. I'd edit his writing when I woke up, ball my eyes out, and then message him and tell him he's a jerk. It's a sibling thing. So, the statement will remain. Because I really do love him. Always will.

Okay…Kananaskis. We drove to the campsite that Matt worked at for Tim Horton's, and because we were a bit early, we got to stop at one of the lakes that he used to frequent with the kids. The water was low, but that didn't stop us from taking a string of ridiculous selfies in front of it. After a couple of snacks, we drove up to the gate at the camp and were let up the long drive to the first building. Soon enough, we were joined by Matt's Kananaskis crew: Kellog, Beanie, Pablo, Tex and Bootsy (but, is he Bootsy at Kananaskis? He's Bootsy at Summit… Hmm). Tex and Bootsy were a tad late because, as Bootsy put it, Tex had a "hot cheese incident." (Also, one of the "Kellog, Beanie, Pablo" folks was not there, but even face-to-face I'm not sure who was who.

My camp names were Lyssy [from Parky] and Red Mama from the kids from Mexico. Suiting and easy to remember). After receiving our very bright green "Visitors" stickers (was Matt really a visitor? In his mind, never.), we toured the campsite so Matt could see how different it was from his time there. The crew recounted so many Matt stories they'd take up another book, I'd bet. Hearing the stories made me feel like I knew my brother at a time when I didn't really know him based on the difference in our ages. What made it more sweet were the photo albums the crew made and gave to Matt. He's a boy-bander, a cross-dresser, and everything in-between in those albums (not a lot of in between there per se, but you catch my drift). They also put together an album with everyone's favourite Matt story. I hope that Carter and Harry get to read these one day...they'll get to see their dad in a way that no one other than these folks can really describe. When it came time to leave, there wasn't a dry eye in the house. The friendships Matt forged at that site were so clear and so powerful. You could tell that this loss was going to stay with them long after driving home from the mountains, and definitely longer than the "hot cheese" on Tex's shirt.

We drove back to Calgary for the last leg of our whirlwind trip to the west. We stayed at the Sheraton Calgary Eau Claire. To absolutely NO ONE'S SURPRISE AT THIS POINT, our room was stacked with treats and one of our biggest hotel take-aways so far: personalized robes. Yup. Matt somehow managed to get this hotel to make us robes with our bloody names on them. Kid had the shining or something. (Side note: Matt ended up writing to this hotel when we got home and asked them to make one for everyone in our family...and THEY DID...because Matt Dean...because he's kind of a big deal). We really just spent the night here before heading to the airport to head home, but we managed to find our last dinner spot just a stone's throw from the hotel. I have one of the last pictures Matt would take with me at this spot — he felt strongly we needed to document that the clubhouse sandwich I ordered that was the size of my head. We sent the picture to Andrew and Josh because siblings.

The next morning before we drove to the airport, we walked across the street to check out a booth set up on the corner selling cowboy hats. Did we buy hats? Of course we did. Did we buy the same hat? Of course we did. Did Matt make me take his picture in front of a cut-out cow backdrop? Of course he did. When in Calgary, right? Our real last stop was a Denny's. I'm mentioning this because despite Matt's diagnosis, he still maintained his sense of humour (always). At breakfast, he insisted on trying to flip the little milk cartons you get at your table for coffee/tea. "Third time's a charm," he said as he doesn't make the carton flip the way he had intended. "I still got it!" he exclaimed as it sped across the table, landing on my lap. "Right in my crotch," I said. "Gross," he laughs. Siblings. His smile is so big, I still see it in my mind.

We landed in Ontario and had to drive back to North Bay from Toronto. We had zero issue with this…know why? Remember when I said that Matt would take one of his last pictures with me of a clubhouse sandwich earlier? Well, he totally redeemed himself on this drive back. With hands as steady as he could make them, Matt captured our personal escort on the 401: the Batmobile. That's right, folks. The Batmobile. The Dark Knight knew we needed supervision, so he followed us as far as Barrie and then determined that North Bay was a little north for his blood. So the rest of the way it was just the two of us. A trip of a lifetime.

Chapter Nineteen

A Trip to the Jays

Written by Joshua Dean

Matt and I had discussions about attending a Blue Jays game in late August, as my job was fairly busy in the early summer. However, Gemma had been monitoring Matt's decline, and reached out and suggested maybe earlier as his mobility was starting to be affected to the point that he might need two people to keep him upright and moving.

We decided on the July 21, and the Jays were playing the Baltimore Orioles. I picked Matt up at the cottage, promising Gemma I would return him only "slightly" damaged, and we headed off in their van, as Matt was getting too weak to be able to haul himself up into my Jeep. Actually, I left our car with Gemma for the boys, as my wife, Sarah, had borrowed my Jeep for an adventure of her own, which bears mentioning for later in the story.

As we headed down, we talked about the endless nothings that siblings normally talked about when stuck together on long trips. We talked about the future of the kids (both mine and his), hockey (no surprise there), and I think a little bit of everything in between.

The trip into Toronto was uneventful, and we had decided I would buy the tickets for the game and Matt would get a hotel room. Of course, Matt decided on the hotel in the Roger's Centre (the SkyDome) partly because we could literally go down the elevator to the level we were at for the game, but also because, well, Matt.

I should point out to the reader at this time that as Matt and I were the oldest, we had been away from home the longest, and so by extension, less involved in each other's lives than our younger two siblings. When I say, "Well, Matt," it was because he had gained a bit of a reputation over the years of being a little more than extravagant. But at the same time, deservedly so. He had earned his money, so I just chuckled to myself and carried on.

We got to the hotel, and had a porter help get our suitcases and park the van underneath the hotel. We got a room facing the street where we could look out at the sea of people attending the game. We had arrived in just enough time to get installed in the hotel room and then head down to see the game. I had chosen tickets along the third base line where it was both as easy as possible for Matt to navigate, but also hopefully be seen on TV if a foul ball came our way. (What can I say, I was hoping to get us our fifteen minutes of fame.) We were able to tuck the wheelchair behind the last row of seats (we weren't supposed to be able to bring it down to the seat level), but the usher looked the other way, and we were grateful.

We watched the game, which was in itself fairly meaningless. I mean, they won, but the season itself was nothing to write home about (sorry Jays). We did head to the Jays store after where we both got Star Wars themed Blue Jay shirts, which we wore the next day to the Hockey Hall of Fame.

After the game was done, we headed a short distance to Wayne Gretzky's for a bite to eat. We had a good meal and some good conversation, and then grabbed some treats from a convenience store and headed back up to the hotel room.

It was at this point that I really got a good look at how much the ALS had started to take hold, as Matt needed to go to the bathroom. I had known it was getting worse, (as we could see when we came out to visit), but I hadn't realised how much it affected him at that point. It was almost a ballet dance to maneuver him onto the toilet. Because the ALS had gone after his hands first, he had to ask me to wipe his bum after he was done, and I realised the trust he had placed on me to take care of him. I got him cleaned up and in bed, and we watched an old movie for the rest of the night.

We got up the next morning and headed down the elevator to the dining room of the hotel where we watched the ground crew cleaning up the Roger's Centre after the game, and getting the field ready for a game later that night. We then packed up the suitcases and headed to the Hockey Hall of Fame. As we toured around, we had a blast talking about the history of the game, as it was probably our strongest connection. Matt was eager to see the international part of the Hall, as one of the teams he coached had a jersey in it. Matt ended up coaching the Singapore National Ice Hockey Team, and one of the defenseman's jerseys somehow ended up in the Hall. Matt was pretty clear that it meant that he was in the Hall of Fame, and I actually agreed. (The reader should know that I am a huge Philadelphia Flyers fan, and Matt was a huge Montreal Canadiens fan, and we both never wasted an opportunity to chirp each other about our respective teams.) We spent the morning moving about the various displays and taking in the history of the old trophies. We even got to touch the Stanley Cup. Probably jinxed it for both of our teams for the next decade at least. But I digress.

After we were done at the Hall, we ventured down the mall that runs along side it and grabbed some McDonald's for lunch. At this point Matt was pretty tired and was ready to go home.

We got back into the van and headed back to North Bay. As we were coming out of Toronto, he kept checking his phone for the LCBO, as he was looking for a special bottle of Japanese whiskey. There was supposedly one bottle left at the Barrie LCBO on Bayfield St., so at his insistence, we made the short detour and I went into check the inventory for him. Unfortunately, there was no bottle left to be bought.

We got back on the road, and as we were coming up to Gravenhurst, I mentioned to Matt that there was a Jeep that looked almost like mine in the lane ahead. As we got closer, I kept looking at the Jeep, thinking, wow, that looks like mine. We got close enough to read the license plate, and it was in fact mine! My wife had picked up her mother and was headed back to a cottage for a week with my youngest two kids, and we had managed to find here on her journey there. Matt and I chuckled about this all the way home, and talked about what an unlikely event it was.

As we pulled into the driveway at his cottage in Sturgeon, I knew this was the last trip we'd make together, just the two of us, and I gave him a great big hug. Not going to say we both cried, but I'm also not going to say we didn't. And that is the story of my brother and I making one last trip together before the ALS took his body away from him.

Chapter Twenty

Return to Oak Island

Written by Andrew and Alyssa Dean

Matt will appreciate what I'm about to write about the most epic, most mysterious, most secretive trip to Oak Island ever made:

.

.

.

.

.

.

Sorry, we signed NDAs. The truth lies with Matt and Matt alone. N44° 30' 44.312152"; W64° 17' 675382". Sempre Avanti.

Chapter Twenty One

Why I Chose to Die

I chose to die for a short, simple reason. I don't want to overstay my welcome. A lot of people that say that sounds ridiculous obviously have never been in the shoes that I currently have on right now. I feel totally helpless and useless. That is a dangerous and difficult combination. No one exactly knows how to deal with this fact of life. However, I get to choose my time and be surrounded by my loved ones. Not a bad trade-off. I am already beyond being fair to Gemma. She has been looking after me full-time since July, and I am eternally grateful for all of her love and attention. She also had to look after Carter and Harrison. We would not have been able to handle all of this so gracefully without the help of everyone else involved, our families, friends, carers, case manager, OT, ALS Society and all the doctors and nurses.

How I want to be remembered and the reason that I am not having a traditional funeral is because death sucks and so do funerals. Have you ever been to a funeral and said, "Wow what a great time." I don't want a Debby Downer funeral. I am going to have a party. One that celebrates not only my life but the people in it and how they helped shape it. I would not have been me without all of the relationships that I was involved in. People need to know how much I cared for and valued them. So, I figure a kick-ass party is the best way forward in death. Plus it will be better money spent than the average cost of a funeral.

What does this all mean? I envision the party starting off with a bagpiper, followed by a shot bar with Russian vodka and whiskey. Maybe some live music; I will ask Davis if he would like to do it. I would ask him to play *Membership*, *Long Time Running*, *Sleeping Sickness*, *In A World Possessed by the Human Mind*, and *Down the Road*. These are some of the songs that we used to play when we got together. What is a party without food? What food should be served? I am thinking of pizza by Arugula, but I don't know if they would. I don't think that the restaurant is big enough for all the people that would come. Not that I am expecting a lot, but it is not that big of a restaurant. The pizzas are amazing though. I would be happy with a place big enough to accommodate guests and catered by Arugula or The Cedar Tree. How could you not like pizza or Shawarma? I would like to be remembered as a kind and caring person. That is all I have ever tried to be.

To say goodbye is never easy but it reminds me of saying goodbye to Amy, my awesome work wife, when she moved to Dubai. We shed some tears and I toasted her and then we all had a shot of vodka. What I said was:

In Singapore, we drink to say goodbye and in Dubai we will drink to say hello.

V Singapure my vypivaem na proshanie, a v Dubae vypiem za vstrechu!

В Сингапуре мы выпиваем на прощание,а в Дубае выпьем за встречу!

I thought it would be classy and cool to do it in Russian since they have been known to toast in many profound ways. It turned out to be pretty boss. So have a drink for me and I will see you on the other side. If there is one. I did ask Jesus to save me in front of Notre Dame in Montreal, but I guess it was not in the cards. Which is why I decided to be an organ donor so I can keep on living. Loophole! Just kidding. I have been an organ donor since I got my driver's license. What am I going to do with them when I die? I may as well give them to someone in need. If I could help someone then I should.

Chapter Twenty-Two

The Last 24

This has nothing to do with Jack Bauer, but I did almost work for CSIS. Or did I work for the Canadian government as a spy? I did live in the Middle East and Russia as well as South East Asia.... Perfect cover as a school teacher. Even in my dying hours I am still pretty funny. ALS continues to take even more, and now it has driven me to my breaking point. I could handle not being able to move that well because the connections are gone between my brain and my body. I have learned to live with constant twitching all over my body. I can even handle the loss of my voice. Even the pain that comes from spasms and the fact that my muscles are shrinking. What I can't handle is losing the ability to go to the bathroom. It was the deal breaker. Gemma has enough on her plate and adding another diaper into the mix is not only unfair but totally unreasonable. I can't expect this of her even though I know that she would do it without thinking because she is selfless. I decided that if it was ALS when everything started I would go when I was bed bound. So here I am. Ready to die and donate my organs to someone else. Why? Why not? If I can help one person is that not worth doing what I am doing? I have been fortunate to live a great life in half the time. Suck on that death.

Matt was able to donate several of his organs to others. We do not know their identities. We do know that someone received Matt's liver, two people each got a new kidney and his eyes were used for research. Matt could not change what was happening to him or his fate, but he wanted to ensure that he could help someone else live a better life with the best gift he could leave behind.

Chapter Twenty-Three

Thank yous

To the amazing CIS community and our friends & family around the world,

I just wanted you to know how much I enjoyed getting to know all of you. I know a lot of time has passed and we haven't spoken for awhile, but that doesn't change how I feel about all of you. I want to thank all of you for your support and kind words. I truly appreciate everything everyone has done to help Gemma and our family navigate the treacherous waters of this devastating disease.

We left Singapore almost a year ago, and we miss it every day. We have been spending time visiting with friends and family, as well as preparing for the arrival of our second child. We thought we would have missed winter, however, winter did not get the memo. We still have snow on the ground. This has been great fun for Carter, who up until this point in his life has never seen snow or been outside when it is cold. Full disclosure, when it hit 20 degrees in Singapore doesn't count. He has thoroughly enjoyed playing in the snow, as have we.

February 28, 2018, changed my life. It was the day I was told by the doctor that I was going to be diagnosed with ALS. I had already known this in my heart, but deep down inside I was hoping that it was going to be something treatable to the extent that I would recover fully. Even though I knew it to be true, I didn't want to hear it. This diagnosis changed everything. It changed how I look at the world and everyone in it. I can no longer take things for granted and I will cherish every moment in life that comes my way.

Mrs. Dean and our families would like to thank the school for the astounding support in helping us return to Canada. We had many concerns about everything, but the leaders of our school looked at us and told us not to worry, that they would take care of everything. And they did tenfold. We could never thank them enough for what they did for us.

CIS has been a magical place for us these past six years. We have been blessed with the opportunity to teach wonderful children who have wonderful parents. We worked with fantastic teachers who we are lucky enough to call friends. We truly appreciate all of the support that the CIS community has given to us. It will allow our family to face this challenge head-on and spend the time I have left together. The kind words and gestures help give me strength that I didn't know was possible.

What words could I use to express our thanks? Kindness? Caring? Love? In the words of the late Jack Layton, "My friends, love is better than anger. Hope is better than fear. Optimism is better than despair. So let us be loving, hopeful and optimistic. And we'll change the world." I know these words to be true because you have all changed ours.

Chapter Twenty-Four

Notes from People about Matt

Written by Various People

1. Chad Denault

Hey Mr. Dean, I'd just like to take this time to thank you for the time you dedicated to my education and well-being as a child. I still remember a presentation I did in your Grade 5 class about my grandfather. The first time my classmates had ever seen me cry. I remember walking over to your desk afterwards and the support I received from you afterwards will always be with me. I'll never forget the time I looked out my math class window to see a herd of Grade 8 children in full sprint chasing after a bald man with a rubber chicken in his hand. One of the many great memories at St. Anne's. Although I will never be a support to your choice of NHL team, me along with all of my St. Anne classmates will forever support you.

2. Cade Darrington

Hey Mr. Dean, just wanted to say our thoughts and prayers are with you, you had one of the biggest impacts on our class's lives and we all wanted to thank you for that. Our thoughts and prayers are with you and your family and congratulations on the new little addition □

3. Taaylor Leon

Hi there,

I don't know if you remember who I am at all, but I used to be a student of yours in Iroquois Falls at St. Anne's years ago. I heard about what's been going on through my mother. She and I both remember you fondly for being the kindest, most helpful teacher I ever had throughout my schooling. We were deeply touched by the news, as we have had two close family members pass from ALS. It can certainly be tough. My mother and I both live in North Bay, and I understand that you are currently staying here with family as well. If it's not too much, I'd like to offer a hand if your family needs anything. Whether it be help with things locally, the baby, etc. Please don't hesitate to let me know.

4. Donald "Odie" O'Dwyer

Dear Monte,

I wanted to apologize for not reaching out to you the moment that I heard about your condition. The truth is that I have been wracking my brain trying to come up with something — anything — to say. The truth is that there is nothing that I could possibly say that could bring you or your family comfort in these times. I have rewritten this email multiple times, rearranging the words in an attempt to perfect what I wanted to say, an effort that amounted to a zero sum. While attempting to string together clever words into fragile and sensitive sentences I began to lose what I was really wanted to say:

I love you, man.

I love you because you moved heaven and earth to make it to my wedding. Through hell, high water and two feet of snow, you travelled a hell of a long way to see me marry the girl of my dreams. Thank you. Your presence there has always meant the world to me, and I am not entirely sure that I ever expressed that to you.

I love you because you taught me my first few chords, and helped me to learn to pretend to play the guitar...I still suck to this day, but those early lessons really helped me get through some difficult times. Thank you.

Danelle and I celebrated our anniversary this year by heading to Banff for the evening, and wouldn't you know we ended up in the Rose and Crown. I told the story of the infamous Jarvina performance from what I could recall from my foggy memories. Monte was the only man on the planet who could drag us all up onto that stage for a live performance...classic. In many ways, you were our own personal Gord.

Your love of this country is something to be admired. Your work within our borders and overseas embodies the true north strong and free spirit that all Canadians strive to represent to the outside world. You are red, white and true, all the way through.

Thank you for letting out your inner nerd with me. The enthusiasm and energy that you put into our Star Wars lightsaber battle was amazing. Not many people would have allowed their eyebrows to be torn out for the sake of a Darth Maul plaster mask (sorry about that). Your commitment and dedication astound me.

You have always valued your friends and family above all else. You have always had the balls to tell the ones that you value the most how much they mean to you. Never afraid to say that you love someone.

Although we have followed differing paths since our days together at the ranch, I often look back on those times with envy. It truly was the best job that I have ever had. But more than that, I was surrounded by people who made me a better person, a fundamental relationship experience that has been lagging in my professional career since those amazing summers. Thinking about the continued differences that you have been able to make in the lives of others fills me with pride and adoration. If you have been able to impart a fraction of your impeccable character and influence on those lives as you had mine, then you have indeed made this world a much better place.

I feel tremendously honoured to have been able to be present during a small fraction of your life, and feel absolutely devastated for those who will not be able to experience the full Monte (you know what I mean).

I know that we have not been a part of each other's lives over the past seventeen years, and for that I am sorry. Friends like you don't come around very often, and not being able to raise my head out of the daily routine of school/work/kids has made me realize that I have let someone amazing pass by. For that, I am sorry my friend.

Monte, I love you, and I am truly heartbroken for you, your family, and selfishly myself.

I love you, man.

Don Odie O'Dwyer

PS:

I would love to talk to you if you feel up to it. Out of country for a week, but always reachable over email.

PPS:

The ring still fits.

5. Shawn Turner

That's pretty sad stuff, buddy. Been sipping cognac for an hour now and I'm beside myself. You are without a doubt the smartest, nicest, just all around best guy I know. I know I try to play my cards tight to the chest, but you've always been someone for me to look up to. When we first met I was a rather lost soul, but you've honestly encouraged me to become closer to who I was before I got lost. You have an amazing spirit, and I'm proud to call you a close friend. You have my complete respect and if there's anything I can do for you or Gemma, just name it. Jen and I will definitely see you in a few weeks. I can't imagine what you're going through. I'm here if you need to talk or anything.

6. Lyndsey Flemming (Alice)

Ahh Matt, I knew on Tuesday something was wrong. In honesty, I've known for a while as you've not been your usual happy self. You'd lost your mojo!

Personally, I will miss seeing you around so much. There are no words to describe what you guys must be feeling. There is so much love and support out there for you, please take some comfort in that. I also want you to know that in years to come when Alice is asked to name that teacher who inspired her, the one she remembers encouraged her the most, she will always name you. You are so loved, Matt, by all your students. You have a true gift, please remember that. Like you said, I will always cherish our friendship and be supporting you and your beautiful family from afar. Xx

7. Maureen Delaney (Peter)

I hope you don't mind me sending this to you but I just read the school's advisory and from the bottom of my heart I am so sorry to learn of this news. You are an incredibly strong individual and I know you will fight this the best that you can. I will miss having you around the school as will Peter. You will be a hard hole to fill for them. Thank you for the laughs and more importantly for all the help and inspiration you gave to Peter...you would be amazed how much of an impact you truly have on these kids. If there is anything that our family can do for your family please, please, please let us know. You and your family are in our thoughts.

Maureen

Hi there... Peter wrote an email to you but we didn't know if you still were using the school account so he is using my fb messenger...

Mr. Dean,

I wanted to write and say that I was sorry to hear the sad news about your family. I really miss having you at school for a lot of reasons. I think I might be the only Habs fan left. Mr. Warford said he would give me "Exceeds Expectations" if I start to cheer for the Leafs…but I told him no. I was happy with sticking with my team and getting "Meets Expectation"!!!

You are one of my favourite teachers and I wish you were still here. I am bringing all Montreal shirts for excursion and will wear them in honour of you!! Miss you and thank you for everything you have done for me.

Peter Evans

8. Melanie Seet (Matthew)

Mr Dean! Geez.

It's been really bothering me since I heard. I've shed some tears. It's also bothered me we didn't get a chance to give u a big hug and wish u all the positivity in the world! So take this as a huge hug from all of us! We aren't family but you made such a huge impact on our lives teaching Matthew last year in G2-6. No one else has ever empowered him to want to achieve his best! I hope you are feeling the love from everyone cos there is a lot! We have supported your Go Fund page and will continue to do so as and when necessary so keep it going!

Would love to send you and your family off at the airport but understand that a quiet exit may be a simpler one. You won't be popping into school anymore, I imagine? Let me know.

Pls keep us posted on your health and we will all keep you in our prayers!

I remember so clearly just jabbering to you in the playground after school when my younger daughter started at CIS Aug/Sept last year. And all the other random times we said hi. I'll also remember "Hands on your head"! Even Charlotte had drawn you a card last year cos that's how we felt about u in this household!

Take care. I know this is an insanely difficult time for u and family. It's also a difficult time too for people like me who know you and find it hard to digest. If there's anything we can do... pls shout.

Sending much love and big hugs!!
Mel, Raj, Matthew & Charlotte Vaswani

9. Vanessa Moore (Victor)

Matt, I just heard the news about your diagnosis. I have no words to express how sorry I am. You have really touched our lives as you are still Victor's favourite teacher ever. If there is anything I can do for you or your family please don't hesitate to let me know. Sending you all lots of love. I can't imagine what you're going through, Matt. I can see from the Gofundme page that you are surrounded by love and support and that Gemma and the kids will always have that too. Please do take me up on it if there's absolutely anything I can do for you.

10. Natalie Bassett (Charlie and Lily)

Oh my God, Matt. That is devastating. I just had to read that again and again for it to sink in. I don't even know what to say to you, "sorry" is not enough. I wish I could be near to help you all through it. Please know that I will stay in touch with Gemma and if she returns to the UK I will help with the children as much as she needs. You are such a shining light and have touched our family in so many positive ways. We will never forget your kindness or commitment to teaching and the fun you brought every day. I am hoping to come to SG in October so please hold on for us. I'm sending you all our love and light at this most awful time. Call me anytime even if you just want to cry. xx

I can't imagine how frightened you must feel. I wish I could help in some way. I know your family will take excellent care of you and your brood though. It will be good to be home and surrounded by love and support.

11. Raye Gibbons (Bella)

Hi Matt, I can't seem to get you and Gemma off my mind so I thought I'd send you a message . I'm sure you are overwhelmed with messages, emails and calls and I don't expect a reply I just wanted you know what a great teacher you have been and what an incredible impact you make on your students, especially Bella. I know I've told you before but you were born to teach ❤□. I will continue to pray for you, Gemma, Carter and your baby boy Dean. Please know if there is absolutely anything I can do for your family before you leave please just ask . Hugs to you all,

Raye

Hey Matt , Renee mentioned that you had your flight this Friday. If you need help with transportation to the airport please don't hesitate to ask. Also, if there is anything you need before you go! Thinking of you all!

Raye

Hi Matt, it's been awhile. Was baking this week and thought about you, first instinct when I took the muffins out of the oven was to run some up to your class □. With you gone it has been been on my waistline as I'm sharing less and eating more □. Hope things are well in Canada and you're enjoying the time with your family. I loved your recent update on the Gofundme page. Hope you're feeling well. Keeping you all in our prayers .

Hey Matt, Bella had her first day orientation today at her new school. She was there with all the new students, she had to say one thing she missed about her old school and she said her favourite teacher, Mr. Dean ❤□

12. Sheri Venedam

I CANNOT even believe the words I just read above! This makes me so beyond sad and I feel so much love for you seeing these pics!!! You are too much of a good person to have such a horrible thing happen! Your life is one that needs to be celebrated! I swear I gave you credit every single time I've ever made Puff Chicken! Lol! I am sending you the biggest hugs I could possibly send. I am praying for you and your family and hoping deeply for a miracle!

13. Natalie Bozic

Thinking of you!!! Xoxo You were always a true friend and "roommate" when living at my dad's! My dad always thought highly of you! He's in Pioneer Manor and has Lewy body dementia. It's been a year on April 21 (his bday)! Time flies! But anyways! I saw that article and thought of you! You have a lot of support and I hope things improve for you!!! Mattttttt xoxoxo!!!! Love Nat

14. Laura Beaulac

Hello friend. I recently heard from Dave over the phone and he shared with me your ALS diagnosis. I wanted to reach out to you to tell you that I am thinking of you and that I can't imagine what you're going through. Big hugs! Any chance you'll be out west, let me know I'd love to show you around. You are the big reason I taught in Japan with JET. It was life-changing. You have that effect on people you know. Very special soul, you are. xoxoxoxo

15. Flavia Blanchard

Dear Mr. Dean,

We heard you are returning to Canada. I just wanted to thank you for the positive impact you have had on Justina — and all of us in fact! — during our first year in Singapore. Such impressions on kids tend to accompany them for life — making them a better person.

We will keep you and your family in our hearts and daily prayers like I know hundreds of students whom you have made better persons will as well.

All our love,

Xxx

Blanchard family

16. Juliette and Pierre (Louis)

Dear Matt,

Words are not enough to tell you how profoundly we are in thoughts with you, Gemma, little Carter, and baby boy to be.

Pierre and I pray for the amazing human being you are. We're with you, we're accompanying you, sending you strength, courage and love.

Very warmly,

Juliette and Pierre

17. Aditya's mom

Mr. Kiddell and Ms. Andrea,

I would like to place on record my appreciation for the level of dedication, commitment, enthusiasm, sincerity and methodical planning which Mr. Dean brings, day after day, to his role in shaping young minds.

I base this feedback on the inputs I receive from my son, Aditya, as well as the numerous opportunities I've had to observe him interact with kids both in the class as well as on field trips.

A few examples of what I've seen:

1. Irrespective of the number of kids vying for his attention, he listens to each child's question with respect and provides them an answer. He also makes sure that he is fair and enforces the rule that children take turns.
2. A couple of cases of inappropriate behaviour in his class that were highlighted to him were acknowledged and action taken promptly. He also got back with the action taken.
3. Aditya is always eager to share what he has learnt in class with me. I notice that he understands the concept being taught really

well and feels proud about what he knew and what he now knows. He also has a lot of respect for Mr. Dean and his words.

4. Instructions to parent volunteers are precise and information is shared well in advance so that the children gain as much as they can from the volunteers' time with them.

Here's wishing Mr. Dean the best.

18. Rob Kiddell

---------- Forwarded message ----------
From: Robert Kiddell <robert.kiddell@cis.edu.sg>
Date: Thursday, May 22, 2014
Subject: Re: Matthew Dean

Dear Natalie,

What a delightful note! And it arrived at a perfect time, as Matt and I just met to discuss a field trip and about how things were going with him. He is a very bright light and we are very lucky to have him. I agree, he is personable, professional, skilled and a super teacher.

I am sorry you are leaving us and wish you, Charlie and Lily all the best.

Thank you so much for writing as it does allow me to express my sincere appreciation to Matt in a, perhaps, more meaningful way.

Cheers,

Rob

Dear Rob,

I just wanted to feedback my thoughts and feelings about Matthew Dean as we are soon to leave CIS for Dulwich, SG.

He taught Charlie (for most of) last year after a teacher was suddenly dismissed and he has taught Lily this year. I have also been room parent for him this year and have spent a lot of time in the classroom, so I feel very well qualified to let you know our experience.

First of all I thought Matt stepped in and took the baton seamlessly, even though I'm quite sure he was as shocked and surprised as we were when we were informed about the departure of a teacher . He certainly was thrown in at the deep end.

From many of the parents perspectives he really saved the day. Were it not for Matt and the way he talked so confidently about the things he could bring to the classroom, we would not have returned to CIS for a second year. I felt so sorry for him being thrown in at the deep end but he didn't seem fazed at all.

Matt has been our ray of light at CIS, he is excellent at communicating with parents, the blog is always up to date, he replies to emails within a couple of hours, without fail, and he is a very pleasant person to be around. He has always been professional and open-minded when it came to issues with behaviour in the classroom or the playground, dealing with any problems quickly and efficiently. He has been helpful and understanding when it came to arrangements with the bus or changes to the children's day because of appointments or illness.

I must be honest and say I have not been a fan of the IB curriculum in the early years, I am sure it is better in latter years but it certainly has not suited my children. That being said, I feel that Matt has done an exceptional job in teaching the children to the best of the IB's parameters. He makes the day interesting, varied and fun, using his background in music and drama to bring the children the best of academics mixed with the arts. He also always sets home learning that is age appropriate and has a variety of tasks that the children can do as much or as little as they can. He understands that sometimes other things get in the way, like ECAs or illness, and he will never make a child feel bad about it but instead give more time to finish if appropriate. He has implemented a sticker reward chart that really seems to motivate the children to want to try harder in class and at home.

He is very good at noticing when a child is out of sorts, and taking time to find out why and feeding back to parents if necessary. The children respect him and look up to him as a strong role model. They also enjoy going to school everyday. In my opinion, there should be more male teachers like Matt, particularly in international schools' early years, as the children often have absent fathers who travel a lot and need a male influence in their lives. In the many times I have worked in the pod or the classroom, Matt has been patient to a fault with the children (and me!). He explains everything carefully and spends one-to-one time with anyone who is finding the work challenging.

I have taken the time to write this email to you in the hope that he will be recognised for his hard work and dedication (even when he had his shoulder operation he was still in touch with parents and planning lessons I believe!) and shown plenty of appreciation. I also filled out an online form where not very many positives came to light, so I wanted to make a special note about Matt in case he was lumped into a negative pile with the rest of the form. Without Matt, I'm afraid our time at CIS would have been a very different story.

I sincerely hope you can take the positive feedback to him, because in my mind, where he has been concerned, there have not been any negatives.

Kind regards,

Natalie Bassett

Rob continued

Hey Matt, how is my favourite teacher when all the others are away! Ha hA. Seriously you are the most honourable teacher I have ever come across. In the most difficult time of my career, dealing with a teacher who was let go, you bailed me out. You took over the classroom and never dwelled, at least in the open, about all the nonsense that went on. Do you remember when the former teacher sent letters to all the students? That you took over mid-year speaks to so much about you. That you never told other teachers of all the nonsense that you went through is so truly remarkable. I am truly honored and ever so lucky to call you my friend. Oh and thanks for all the chats about hockey. I question the two of us make a formidable team…well you are the strength but I would try try to cling to your jersey. Keep smiling Matt and thank you for seeing me through a very very dark time. You are the best!

My reply

Thank you for your kind words. I truly appreciate them. You put your faith in me and I could not let you down. It was not easy and I would not wish it on anyone. That being said, your support throughout that difficult transition was just what I needed. I don't have much time left but your message has made this easier. Thank you for believing in me and trusting that I would be up to the job.

Rob's reply

Well, if you are shuffling off to the hockey rink in the sky, I can only hope that you will let me play on your team. Cuz it will be fun, humorous and incite lots of passion. But I'm not a guy who ever loses hope. So I hope for the best for you and I hope that any journey you take is delightful and awe inspiring. You, as I have said too many times, are a Star. And I still owe you…ha ha

19. Tyler

Hey buddy,

Just wanted to tell you that I think of you every day and when things are getting tough at work there is so much you taught me. I was a new teacher and you took me under your baby hook throwing arm and showed me the way. You are an inspiration and I am such a better teacher thanks to your guidance. I hope u are fighting away man!! Miss you and love you!!

20. Ariel Yuan

Dear Mr Dean,

Hi, I'm Ariel Yuan from your second grade class in 2012. I got this email account from Terry's mom and I was just hoping to email you & check-in with you. How are you doing? I hope you and your family are having a wonderful Christmas, and that your condition is improving drastically. I'm writing this email from sunny Vancouver as I am on holiday here with my family. When I heard Terry has gone to visit you in Toronto I wanted to visit myself but our family is going back to Singapore soon.

I don't know much about your condition just that you have a disease called ALS. I've been doing some research on people with the same condition like Stephen Hawking and other less famous people like Steve Wells who lived in Toronto as well as Chris Pendergast from New York and I've noticed a trend in their behaviours that differs them from many others. I've realised that being positive is one of the most important things in surviving this ordeal, allow me to explain. The three people I've listed all lived with ALS for more than two decades (with Stephen living with it for more than five). After doing some research, I came to the conclusion that all three of them had something in common that affected their condition deeply: their positivity and their determination to live their life no matter their condition. As you probably know, Stephen was very celebrated in science and has made many astounding discoveries despite his restraint in mobility and speech; Steve Wells, though not as famous, once said "I have a terminal illness…so what?" and according to him he "accepted the diagnosis immediately and I've continued to live life to the fullest, taking ALS along for the ride." Chris Pendergast founded the non-profit organisation Ride For Life that raises money for research involving those with ALS. They all decided to push on in their times of despair. I know staying positive must be very hard through your condition, but maintaining a healthy mindset will always help no matter the situation.

And now for the sappy stuff…Mr. Dean, you were one of the best teachers I ever had. You were fun, welcoming and never seemed to be mad. I really hope that you and your family are well and that your condition will improve more and more with each passing day. No need to write a long response to this email as I know it must be very difficult to write with your eye movements only , just please give me your account number. My family and I would like to give you a small token of our deepest empathy as soon as we get back to Singapore. Have a great holiday!

Sincerely,

Ariel

21. Lise Turner

It's not always easy to say what is in our hearts. But on the ride home all I could do is think of you. You came into our lives and found your spot in our hearts. It was as if it was waiting for you. Then you became friends with Shawn, which made our hearts smile. Loved when you two got together. You found your Gemma and that made us happy for you. Then your beautiful boys. I wish I could make you better but I know I can't and that makes my heart cry. We love you, Matt, like one of our boys and you will always be in our hearts.

22. Amy

I know you have important things and I don't want to take up time…And I am not good at this…I don't know how to say goodbye to you. And I know I am not a good enough writer to explain how much I value our friendship or how lucky I feel that you are a part of my life or the influence you have had in it. So please know you mean the world to me, you are one of the best people I know and the world is going to be a little suckier without you in it. Please know I am going to spoil your boys every chance I get (and Gemma;)) and tell them stories of your awesomeness. I love the memories we have created because when I think about you it makes me feel like you aren't a billion miles away. So on that premise…Say hi to Gord, save me a seat at your jam session (because we all know you two will rock it out) and I will bring the dill pickle chips, two bite brownies, Diet Cokes, Japanese whisky (for you) and bubbles (for me) for the next time we meet…deal?

Thank you for being one of my best friends.

I love you!

23. Mellies

I'm not sure if you will read this, but I wanted to send you so much love. Thank you for making Gemma one of the happiest wives around. Supporting her and your family though so much.

For creating two such beautiful humans whose spirits will always resemble yours and live on within them. Who will feel your heart beating in their own, and know they had a dad who loves them more than words can describe.

For caring so much about the students you have had an impact on all over the world.

Matt, I am very sad to see you leave us, and I know that this has been quite a journey for you. Sending you the biggest awkward hug. Thank you for being exactly who you are and leaving those of us behind with beautiful memories.

xx Melanie

24. Nellie

Dearest Monte,

I want you to know how much you meant to me in those early years of our lives at camp. You were always accepting and giving of love. You will be remembered in my heart. And will always be an example of how to accept others and love unconditionally. Know that you have made a huge impact on all who knew you. May you Rest In Peace knowing that. Thank you, Monte, for being a shining light on this earth. Sending you love on your journey. ❤□

Love Nellie.

25. Sparky

Hello friend. I just want you to know that you have touched my heart and it will always be full when I think of you. Your singing, your guitar, your smile, your amazing hugs. Thank you for being such an amazing person in this world. I will hold you and yours in my heart and prayers for tomorrow. Goodbye my friend. Thank you for all the fish!!

26. Mad Dog

Hey Monte,

I want you to know that you are a big part of what made that Tim Horton Ranch summer memorable for me. It was a hard summer for me after leaving my old beloved camp and you drew me in despite my reluctance. You, my friend, are an includer. You know how to make each person feel special and as if they belong. It isn't just your warm smile, genuine enthusiasm, hilarious antics, charismatic personality and willingness to listen. There is something indescribable about you. Any time that I saw your name on Facebook, I always smiled just thinking about you.

I tell my kids all the time that the most important thing in life is to be kind. You had this nailed and took it to a whole new level. The kids in your groups and classes have had an experience that they will never forget. I hope my kids have a counsellor or teacher just like you.

Thanks for the nickname. I can't say Mad Dog without smiling. It is the best nickname that I have ever had (and probably ever will).

Monte, I am so sorry that life has been unfair to you and you have suffered this horrible illness. The world needs more people like you in it. You inspire me to reach out to include others more and be unabashedly myself.

Love, Mad Dog

27. Solo

Love you bro. A very brave decision your making for tomorrow and I'm proud of you. It must be so hard in so many ways…You are in my prayers and thoughts and I'm giving you a virtual hug right now with tears in my eyes…

You always were a beam of light for me and it was a joy to be in your company. I regret not visiting you when you were in Singapore, and I'm sorry I couldn't make it out to Whistler when you were down last. All regrets aside, I'm honoured to be part of your life and proud to be your friend. Hope to see you in our next life or in the cosmos, whichever comes first. Love you man, may you be at peace.

28. Kix

Hey Monte! So Tex shared the news about your date for assisted suicide. I'm sorry for not reaching out sooner when I heard you were diagnosed with ALS, and during this time for you and your family.

Well shit, Monte. All this really sucks. But you know that.

I want you to know that the two summers I worked at the Tim Horton's Ranch really were two of the best summers. And you were a huge part of that. I could list a number of things/times/stories but what jumps to mind first is how you did not give up on that white kid from Quebec that was so racist and got off the bus calling the black kids niggers. Your compassion, empathy and ability to preserve and see the good in him was something I'll never forget. Thank you for teaching me.

And I remember you coming from Ottawa when I went to Montreal — I think in like 2004 or so. I was there just for fun before a family wedding in the Toronto area and you made a point of coming to see me because Ottawa was "close by." That was fun. □

I believe in God and heaven. I'm not sure where you fall in line in terms of being religious, but I believe you will be up there watching over those that you love and love you. Not sure exactly how to sign off…so

I'll just say that my live has been immensely better and fuller for having you in it. Xox Joanna

29. Crazy

Hey Bro! You are the only person in which all my memories are from happy events. We only had good times. I guess that's the type of people we are. We wanted to do stuff together because we knew it was always going to be fun. Think about it. How many people would find having furniture fly out of their trailer on a busy highway fun, or chasing deranged kids through the wilderness fun, or setting the car in which they are driving on fire, fun. I love you Bro, and I'll cherish all these memories and make sure to share them as well.

30. Ashlee

Matt, just wanted to let you know how much Tom and I love you, and how grateful we are for having met up with you in Perth. Every single memory I have of you is such an amazing one, and I'll never forget the love, respect and admiration you have for Gemma — you are her biggest fan and supporter. I'll also never forget your kind and giving nature, always helping your family and friends.

Big love,
Ash

31. Gerbil

Monte, I just heard the news from Chris. I didn't realize how fast the disease had progressed. I just wanted to tell you that I have the most amazing memories of us at camp. You always brought joy and laughter every day and made everyone live in the moment. I'll miss your sense of humour, warm heart and belly laugh that came right from your soul. AP forever dude. Love you buddy

32. Reese

Monte, I have been reading all the messages from people who love you and, I can't help but be in awe. What a beautiful, meaningful mark you have left on us all, on so many. Thank you for being you, and for sharing your kindness and courage. Love to you and your family.

34. Kellogg

Hello Friend. I am at a bit of a loss here, still processing what Chris shared. What does one say to someone who is leaving this life far too soon? How do I convey just how fortunate I feel to have spent such a formative time in life with you? Our days together, though long ago, still feel very close to the core of who I am today. You lived well this life. You were living well and helping others do the same when I first met you. In having the opportunity to stay connected, I have seen that you've continued to live well and help others do the same throughout your life. To say you have made your mark is an understatement. Your positive impact on me and countless others will persist, and in that way, you will still be here. Your smile, your giggle, your compassion and warmth, your humour, your music, your joy — the full Monte. May your family find comfort in knowing how loved and respected you are by so many. Thank you for the good times. Thank you for being you. Thank you for the full Monte.

35. Odie

Monte,

Odie here (using Danelle's account once again).

I can't even begin to imagine the immeasurable strength and perseverance that you have been able to muster day in and day out. Your bravery, strength and courage have me at a complete loss for words. I am in complete awe of you. Thank you for every moment that you spent with me, thank you for every second that you shared with all of us through your difficult journey. Every minute that you dedicated to others made our lives richer for having experienced just a fraction more of the Full Monte. I am proud to count myself as one of the lucky few who were fortunate enough to cross through your life journey, by luck or fate. Even if only for a moment, the impression that you left will remain with me forever. I love you man. Thanks for being so fucking awesome.

36. Ziggy

Buddy, this is one of the hardest things I've ever written, you're my first friend to be going on your way to the next step! I thought we had more time, I wanted to come up and see you with Cheeks. Interestingly I am in Calgary, on my way to Canmore. I haven't been since we were there at camp together. Michele surprised me with a birthday trip out here, so Toby and my dad came out as well. I'll never forget going to Ottawa, I'll never forget your visit to Japan, and of course our time at camp. Damn dude this hurts. Wishing you a pain-free exit, and your amazing family will carry on your legacy of kindness, compassion and a shit tonne of fun! You're one of the rare ones man. Fuck this sucks.

37. Soomin

Matt, you've come so far on this extremely challenging path. I am so proud of you my friend. I admire the courage you had to go to the hospital and get testing in Singapore, the courage to wait for the results, the courage to face and go through the pain everyday, not for yourself but for Gemma, Carter and Harrison. You are a teacher not only to your students, but also to me. I've learnt the values of selflessness and genuine warmth through you. I am so grateful that we've crossed paths, and that I've had a chance to get to know you and work with you at CIS. I love you, Matt.

Chapter Twenty-Five

Notes I Wrote for the Boys and Gemma

For My Boys - Carter and Harrison

How much I love you and how much I wish that I could be there for you while you grow up will never fade. I have loved every minute of getting to be your dad. I smile just thinking about it. My heart aches when I think about Friday and what that will mean for you. I will go to the hospital and not come back and it is the hardest decision I have ever had to make. One that I never thought I would have to make or want to make. But here we are. Your mother will be able to answer your questions about this and let me tell you how much you're loved.

Carter, I will always remember the night you were born because your mom and I were so excited to meet you. I love how you have grown from a little baby into a wonderful little boy who is curious, kind, helpful, funny and smart. The list goes on. I am so proud of you already and a little jealous that your mom gets to see what you will grow up to become. I love how much you love Harrison. How you want to help care for him and how you love to help your mom. I really enjoyed all of the times that we watched hockey or played it together. I loved to read to you and sing to help you fall asleep. I have created a folder in my Google Drive with the songs that you liked. I'm not surprised that you love Johnny Cash because I do and so does Nonie. At one point it was the only thing that I could sing to calm you down when you were crying. I will forever dream about those moments in my heart. I love you forever.

Harrison, you are the happiest little baby boy that I have ever met and I get to say that I am your dad. Don't get me wrong, Carter was a super-happy baby too, but you have a smile that lights up our hearts and Carter's. Do you know that one of Carter's favourite things to do is make you laugh and he is a professional at it? He makes you laugh more than your mom and I. Because of my ALS, I didn't get to hold you as much as I wanted but I can tell you that you are a great little snuggler. I loved having you snuggle on my chest. I wish that I could hold you once more and never let go. I love you forever.

I have created a treasure chest for both of you. It is full of things for you that meant something to me. Your mom has the videos explaining what they are. There are two other boxes with clothes for you. In case your mom forgets whose is whose, Carter, your box has my CCCP jersey in it. I have quite a few hockey jerseys. I am also leaving you both my movie collection so that you can learn more about me. What I thought was funny or moved me to tears. You can learn a lot about a person by the movies they keep. I hope that you love to play hockey together as much as I did with your uncles. I am sure that your aunt will tell you about how she was the best athlete, but I never saw her make it rain on the basketball court like your old man did. I hope that you treasure these items and that they bring you closer to me.

Wife of a Lifetime

To my darling sweet Gemma, where should I begin? I am so sorry that you had to deal with this. I was really thinking that I would be the one who would look after you in our old age. It was something that I was looking forward to because I love you so much and it would have meant that I had lived my dreams. Being with you was living the dream of all dreams and I never wanted to wake up. It pains me to no end to leave you this way. I wish it was different but it didn't turn out that way. Life has a funny way of kicking you right in the bum hole when you least expect it. You have handled this shituation with grace and an extraordinary amount of love. I want you to know how much I cherish you and love you.

I Will

I will promise to love you with all of my heart,
I will cherish our great times together,
I will remember our funny jokes that were ours and ours alone,
I will long for the touch of your hand and pulling you close to me,
I will wish that I could hold you and caress you once more,
I will never forget how much you made me want to be better,
I will tell you how much I already miss you,
I will sleep soundly knowing you will be there for our children,
I will miss everything about you,
I will miss your lips pressed to mine,
I will miss the warmth of your embrace,
I will miss how happy you made me,
I will miss our adventures around the world,
I will miss not being there for you and our sons,
I will miss growing old with you,
I will miss telling you everything will be alright,
I will miss your beautiful face,
I will love you until the last breath,
I will always love you.

I know that you will do an amazing job raising the boys because you are amazing. Oh my Poops, I am truly sorry for this and for not being able to be there for you, Carter and Harrison. Please take some solace in knowing that you made my life complete and I feel privileged that I got to spend my last ten years with you. I love you forever.

All I Want is You

When I first saw you, I didn't know what to do,
When we started, I had to know,
What was happening and where we would go,
I dreamed I was kissing you,
Feeling my love for you,
Holding on to your lips with mine,
Put me on cloud nine,
Running my fingers through your hair,

Showing you that I cared,
Was the sweetest dream to come true,
The life between me and you,
We mask everything to escape uncertainty,
Especially feelings that absolve all pleasantries,
I listen to you shout at your favourite place,
I wait for the echo to come back and kiss my face.

I Love You

I know you,
I read you like a ten cent comic book,
Classics illustrated,
Romeo and Juliette ,
I sit by my favourite tree,
The wind blows the pages over,
It's almost hands free,
We share the same favourite star,
No matter where we are,

I know I loved you,
I know I loved you,
I know I loved you,
I know I loved you,
I love you.

I read your old letters,
And I can still hear your voice,
Calling out my name,
But it isn't the same,

I know I loved you,
I know I loved you,
I know I loved you,
I know I loved you,
I love you.
I love you,
I love you,
I lovc you,.

Fall Asleep

Hush little baby,
Don't say a word,
You can buy a mocking bird,
The diamond ring,
That's in your eyes,
Sparkles like the stars in the sky,
Snuggle your pillow,
Like the weeping willow,
Cradles the ground,

Fall asleep, baby,
Fall asleep, in my arms,
Fall asleep, baby,
Fall asleep in my arms,

If the wind blows,
Let the cradle sway,
Dance on the breeze until the day,
Light comes in,
From the window pane,
Waking you like a gentle rain,
Loving you,
Is to be,
Because I love you and you love me,

Fall asleep, baby,
Fall asleep, in my arms,
Fall asleep, baby,
Fall asleep in my arms,

One more time,
I'll play for you,
Just to show that I love you,
Sing with me,

When the sun is gone,
When you are too old for this song,
Will you remember?
How you felt,
When we sang our song.
When we sang our song.

Fall asleep, baby,
Fall asleep, in my arms,
Fall asleep, baby,
Fall asleep in my arms,

Chapter Twenty-Six

A Final Note to My Family

Where to start? First of all, I don't want to die without you knowing how much I love you. You are the reason that I am who I am. Someone has to take the blame...I mean acclaim. I love you so much and it pains me to know that we will not get to grow old together. I will get to be remembered as a young man who was at the height of his shiny head and not have to worry about growing old and having a saggy bum that requires a bumbra, while you will have to face the fact that you will not look as good as me on your deathbeds. Too soon?

I am so grateful to Mom and Dad for giving me the three best friends that you ever did see. I knew that I could always count on you for a hug, a kind word, a beat down, or whatever it was that I needed, you would be there. Alyssa, you are without a doubt the best sister we could have asked for and I couldn't have done the west coast trip without you. Your tough exterior isn't fooling anyone and this is why you are our choice for the boys should anything happen to Gemma. Andrew, we have had some great adventures and I am so sad that we won't have anymore. We always have had a great time, even though I was not the best brother growing up. I am so proud of how you love your own family and that you are doing all that you can to give them a great life. I have a secret to tell you, you already did. Josh, you are a great big brother and I learned a lot from you growing up. The most important was being patient and kind to others. You have always been there to move me all over Ontario for work and I appreciate it. Here is to yous, ya filthy animals.

To my mother, we all get our strength from you. You are the strongest human we know and you have the energy of ten people. You have taught us so much about how to be a good person and how to treat others. We really owe you. Feel free to collect from Josh, Andrew and Alyssa at any time. Carter and Harrison are so lucky to have you in their lives and take good care of yourself so that they have you as long as possible. Thank you for all of the sacrifices that you made so we could have a great childhood. It really was the best and I hope that Carter and Harrison get to have something similar.

I love you.

Chapter Twenty-Seven

The Green Ninkies and a Note to Matt, Gemma, Carter and Harrison

Written by Grandma (Betty Dean)

Why? I have asked myself why would Matthew insist in capturing this ancient history? The episode occurred when he was quite young, maybe age three, and we lived in Callander. My brother Fred had offered to take Matthew fishing. The excursion was aborted early because Matthew insisted on coming home early to use the bathroom. None of us could keep a straight face when he emerged from the bathroom to triumphantly announce, "Green Ninkies!!" Perplexed, I opened the bathroom door to examine the toilet contents and was shocked to see green fluorescent floating feces! None of us know what Matthew had ingested that day in terms of food or fluids to produce such unusual results (or the effect it had on Callander's ancient sewage system).

We are, however, forever grateful for zero recurrence.

A note from Betty

Dear Matthew (and I do mean Dear),

This is a letter of love for you
And Gemma
And Carter
And Harrison

Some of it is recollection and some of it reflection and it certainly won't capture you and our forty years together, but I wanted you and your family to have these memories to share and shed some tears over as I am doing while I write this.

In 1978, the most vivid recollection of your birth was delivering you while a nurse in the hallway told my nurse she had lucked in with the cream puff case with Dr. Eckler (her patient's doctor was a late show). Dr. Eckler and your dad debated your birth weight and overcalculated. The nurse told them they were both wrong and you weighed no more than six pounds — and the scales said 5.15 ½. (Savvy nurse!)

Joshua was so excited he couldn't stop hugging and kissing you (I know, hard to believe the day he lost patience with you and said, "No more Mr. Nice Guy" and then decked you).

You were also the most carried of four babies. You had colic and I had to chase Joshua constantly so you spent most of your early days in a snuggler attached to my shoulders.

We moved to Callander by the time you were a year old. You wasted no time falling into the pool (before it had been cleaned, drained and refilled — think swamp water). I had to jump in and pull you out, give you to Nonie who was visiting to run a warm bath and clean you up while I went back to retrieve your rubber boots because Joshua was planning to jump in pool to save them.

Of course you displayed determination from a very early age — the best example being what to wore to Kelly's wedding. Joshua was the ring bearer so I chose a complementary outfit for your debut at the wedding — short pants and matching T-shirt (it was summer). But you threw a royal tantrum and insisted on wearing winter-weight corduroy overalls. Grandma Dean catered to you and you rode to the wedding in their car — gloating all the way!

You probably have more pleasant memories of nursery school than I do. I remember taking Dustin to the back of the room to order him not to ever hit you again — don't think that hindered your relationship with one another.

Janet Bucci told me at a parent teacher interview that you were the child who would remember my birthday — Mother's Day…still waiting (just kidding!). And as I noted at your wedding, my favourite memory was five-year-old Matthew asking me to dance to Louis Armstrong's *What a Wonderful World.*

Given your interest in music, I tried to upgrade keyboards and eventually to a piano. Do you remember trying to play Bryan Adams' *Everything I Do,* and crying in frustration?

Around age five, you required surgery and told me you would commit suicide. That prompted a special tour of the hospital and nursing staff meetings complete with videos and colouring books to explain at child level what to expect. Now I have no idea what thoughts were roaming in your mind, but not even Joshua who had the same surgery could persuade you to look at the bright side. He told you, "You just go to sleep and when you wake up, Mom and Dad are there with new toys for you!" The only clue we got came after we got you home and upstairs to your bedroom. You walked across the hall to the TV room and declared, "I can walk I can walk!" So we were left to deduce you had some erroneous thought you might not walk again.

Both you and Josh were prone to croup and hospitalizations, but you carried it to the extreme ending up being admitted at age twelve (the doctor of the day was under investigation so I ended up staying by your bedside when he made his rounds).

And of course there was the year I had you in emerge once a month for numerous injuries e.g., your nose (did you know Dr. Arthurs is still in emerge and rescued Josh's face from the lost teeth hockey injury and Alyssa during tonsillectomy?). It's still a mystery to me how you could break your knee in mid-air doing the high jump and how you could break an inner bone in your shoulder at hockey and not break the outer bones. At any rate, I paid my parking dues for you at the old hospitals.

Not sure whether I spent more time cheering for you in hockey rinks or at baseball fields. I am sure your baseball coach won't forget calling you in from the outfield to catch at home plate and stopping play when the ball made a loud thud on your plaster cast on your leg!

I know I won't forget the hockey trip to Sault Ste. Marie when I left you in charge of Alyssa at the hotel while I had lunch with my friend, Liz. When I got back — no sign of Alyssa. And then I saw her — just a blur in the water slide. She was not eligible by age or weight but someone with a heavy foot on the scale upgraded her weight!!

You were a wonderful big brother when Alyssa was a baby — you would hold her and walk around the living room and dining room saying, "She just likes to pace." Not so sure you were so generous with Andrew!

I won't bore you with how proud I was that you pursued French Immersion and the ST21 program at West Ferris or all the minor sports interests you had. Or even your years at Laurentian University and the Lakehead. What evolved in this time frame was the four of you conspiring to acquire Hershey and how he became your steadfast friend and confidante — really Matthew, how many people create a stamp with their dog's image on it or take their dog on world travels (except, of course, when you left Hershey with me or Nonie)?

I am so glad you had all those experiences and friendships associated with not just university life but Katimavik, Tim Horton's, Kananaskis and Camp Summit. Your impact on all your friends is so enduring, and I hope that provides you with some peace of mind.

Your world travels — Japan, Bahrain, Moscow, Singapore — have so enriched your life and by extension your immediate family. One of my favourite memories is you sitting in your grandparents' living room in Powassan and sharing your experiences with Pop Pops and Nonie (probably fair return for keeping watch over you on your cycling/ camping trips to the farm).

This is probably the best time to share how proud I was of you delivering the eulogy at Pop Pops' funeral (aided and abetted by your siblings).

We have shared some wonderful family moments (and some not so wonderful).

Thanks for bartending at Josh's wedding in Port Hope. I especially liked my dance with you! I remember asking the DJ to play Tina Turner, *Simply the best, better than all the rest* for your Aunt Gloria. Remember taking her to Ottawa when you were with Katimavik? We hit the mall and you did your usual "hamburger" instead of a traditional Christmas dinner!

I also recall a trip to Ottawa to visit you where your Aunt Kay provided very expensive chocolates for Alyssa, and while we were out having breakfast, Hershey wrecked everything and devoured all the chocolates — I never did tell Kay the fate of those chocolates!!

On a much sadder note, I want you to know how much I appreciated your phone call from Japan in 2002 when your dad decided to leave. I felt so badly for you to be so far away and worrying about everyone back home. But we all persevered and found how resilient we can all be in a time of crisis.

Since then we have all had the joy of welcoming Connor and Alex and Zach into our lives and more recently Mackenzie, Carter, Dax and Harrison, which allowed us all to see you develop as an uncle and father. Do you recall us dubbing you "Uncle Travelling Matt" of *Fraggle Rock* fame?

I want to repeat my gratitude for your support when Pop Pops died in 2007, especially for assisting Nonie to travel to Halifax by train, finding a chauffeur to tourist her around, ensuring she had lobster, and helping set up the family reunion at the Chateau Laurier. Her few short trips to your cottage at Sturgeon Falls were a highlight for her as her health and mobility declined.

I will always treasure the time you and I spent in England in 2011 prior to your wedding and on my retirement from Cambrian College. I don't think there are words to express how wonderful it was to share the history, the beauty of the English countryside or how much territory we covered in a few days. Crazy Canucks in the pouring rain at changing of the guard; security threats to remove us because you took pictures of General James Wolfe crypt; your refusal to join standing ovation waiting for *Bohemian Rhapsody*; walking the spit at Lyme Regis; the Tower of London; lunch in Bristol; visiting Gemma's school; getting jet lag and dozing off in Gemma's flat in Crewkerne; and my favourite, the Churchill War Rooms. Oh, and you are forgiven for criticizing my framing of the tea towels that remind me of Bath. Love the history attached to all of the pubs and how generous Gemma's family was to maximize my time there.

You are a very blessed and lucky person Matthew to choose a December wedding date — Central Park, New York City in 2011 — and have the weather cooperate the way it did. That's what I call attention to detail. Well, actually the true blessing is welcoming Gemma into our family.

I am, in retrospect, so glad we could afford to be there as a family and grateful to Wanda's husband Terry whose travel agency took care of every detail so we could enjoy our short stay as much as we did.

I also want to thank you for guiding your siblings on their UK trip — the best investment I ever made was withdrawing my RRSP to help fund their travel with you. I love all of you so much and in hindsight so much value for such a paltry amount of money.

The hardest part for me was your time in Singapore and not being able to go there when Carter was born, so thank you for "Facetime."

2018 has been devastating for all of us, and I won't ever pretend to know how it has impacted you and Gemma and your two wonderful sons. I just know I cry every day and if I could exchange my life for yours, I would in a heart beat. You now know about parental love first hand so you know how I feel. I promise you this: as long as I live, I will help Gemma and Carter and Harrison however I can.

Know this — your brothers and sister displayed their love and support this spring and summer and they too will be there always. Think "He ain't heavy he's my brother."

You have been incredibly brave and loving in all the mementos you have created for Carter and Harrison.

One of my beliefs is that love never dies. I will always love you, Matthew — you have enriched my life made me a better mom and more importantly a grandmother. Whatever my failings, know I really tried hard to do what's right.

When I was at university, my roommate gave me a copy of Khalil Gibran's *The Prophet*. It's fifty years almost since the gift but I return to it often to try and make sense of what is happening. The two I return to most often are:

Speak to us of Children
And
Speak to us of Death (I read this at my father's graveside service)

Perhaps I should have focussed more on Joy and Sorrow... and then I recalled when my favourite Uncle Jim died:

"and ever has it been that love knows not its depth until the hour of separation"

Chapter Twenty-Eight

Three Days before My Death I Shared This With Tex, Cheeks and Hamlet

Their responses: 6: 19 AM Cheeks

@Monte I love it. Perfect.

Real. Simple yet worldly and tying together all the places and cultures that have touched your life.

I can only imagine what you are thinking and feeling right now. Your situation has made me grateful for my health and acutely aware that my life has been quite sheltered and free of suffering.

I love the party. A celebration of your life and the people in it. A chance for us all to share and relive Monte stories in person. Even if we haven't met.

I understand what you are doing and have tremendous respect for how you have handled this whole process.

I love you buddy.

Tex

Hey Monte, we support whatever decisions you make here. I have not been in your shoes, and I would bet that what I imagine it to be like is not very close to the reality of the situation. You don't have the luxury of hope that you will get out of this one, but like you say, you do get to choose how you ride it out. I know that you have considered everyone involved in this, and I appreciate you sharing your thoughts with us as well, and for asking for our opinions.

I think the party idea sounds very Monte. I like it. These things are as much about commemorating those that we love as with helping us to get a grip on and process our emotions. What does Gemma think of it all? In terms of your planning are you thinking in days/weeks/months?

I'm with Jarvis in that seeing you and reflecting on your situation daily gives me pause to consider how lucky I have been in terms of my own health, and how important it is not to waste time. I feel like you always understood the importance of not wasting time. You have led by example in this sense for as long as I have known you, and you continue to do so. Much respect.

Hoping you can feel the love from Hong Kong

8:15 AM Hamlet

Relationships do shape so much about who we are, don't they?

So we just got a new kitten, and it took us two day to try to reach a consensus as to what to name her. London was pretty mild the other day and I was down by the river watching it flow. Reflecting on our orange, grey with specks of yellow kitten and watching the river the connection came to me, "Bring on the butterscotch, river over spilling its banks." Butterscotch is the name of the kitten. Even at that moment, I thought of you because that is what that song does. Countless connections all over the place to the people we love and that was one of them. Now you are forever connected to my kitten!

Love the party idea. The whole idea of a celebration of life is wonderful. Very Irish! (And Russian apparently.) I'm glad you asked me to play in front of these boys because I would have just showed up with my guitar and insisted that, "I'm sure he would have wanted me to play!" Now it's legit! The song selection is perfect and I would be honoured to play.

Chapter Twenty-Nine

Places Where We Have Been and My/Our Love of Food

Places we have been:

1. Russia - Moscow
2. Scotland - Aberdeen and Logie Coldstone
3. England - Many places
4. Italy - Venice
5. France - Paris
6. Canada - Toronto, Iroquois Falls, Timmins, Cochrane, North Bay, Callander, Powassan, Sturgeon Falls, Sudbury, Mississauga, Montreal, Laval, Ottawa, Burlington, Kingston, Niagara-on-the-Lake, Niagara Falls, St Catharines
7. USA - NYC, Las Vegas, Niagara Falls
8. Wales - Barry Island
9. Singapore
10. Indonesia - Bali, Bintan, Batam
11. Vietnam - Hanoi, Saigon
12. Cambodia - Phnom Penn, Angkor Wat/Siem Reap
13. Malaysia - Malacca, Sean's House, Penang, Langkawi
14. Taiwan - Kenting, Taipei
15. Thailand - Bangkok, Krabi, Phuket, Phi Phi Islands, Chiang Mai
16. Australia - Melbourne, Sydney, Cairns, Perth, Margaret River
17. Philippines - Boracay
18. Hong Kong

19. U.A.E. - Dubai and Abu Dhabi
20. Ireland - Dublin
21. New Zealand - Auckland, Rotorua, Hobbiton, Hamilton, Wellington, Christchurch, Hanmer Springs, Akaroa

Where I have been before your mom or without your mom. The States, Japan, Jamaica, Cuba, Norway, Bahrain, Czech Republic and the Netherlands.

Food that I loved to eat and food that I liked to make. My own recipes:

This part is all about what I liked to eat wherever I lived. So let's get started. Now I have a lot of great food in this part of my life from all over the world. I don't think I will go into a lot of detail and maybe just list my favourites, in no particular order. To be clear, the other countries I have listed will deal with the food that I would have only ate there and not anywhere else. Also, I will tell you the best food that I ate in all of the countries that I lived in and travelled to with and without your mother.

<u>Canada</u>

- Butter tarts and Nanaimo bars — really anything made by your grandma
- Banana Bread
- Steak
- Potatoes any way
- Cheesecake all kinds
- Shawarma from the Shawarma Palace in Ottawa or The Cedar Tree in North Bay
- Burgers
- Poutine
- KD and homemade mac N cheese
- Sour keys
- Popcorn
- All Canadian chocolate bars
- Granola and yogurt for breakfast

- Mini-Wheats all kinds
- Fruit Loops, Lucky Charms, Shreddies, Shredded Wheat, Honeycomb, Alpha Bits
- Pancakes and French toast
- All vegetables and fruits
- Anything Italian!
- La Piazza pizza grecos, Toppers, and arugula, the best pizza I have ever had in Canada was at Badali's in Toronto
- My mom's stir fried rice
- Spanish rice
- Canadian Chinese food especially Sam's parents at the Phoenix in Callander and Ronny Yu's parents restaurant in Iroquois Falls (The Silver Grill)
- Olindo'z Pizza owner, Pat, for making a pizza that was tasty in accordance with ministry guidelines so I could give it to kids at school
- Cabbage rolls
- Chili
- Hot dogs from Maple Leaf Gardens
- Twiggs breakfast
- Perogies any way
- Alberta beef
- Tim Horton's doughnuts and timbits, Canadian maple was my favourite
- Grandpa Dean Turner's fish and chips
- Grandma Lise Turner's moosemeat pie and desserts, especially turtle cake
- Supersata
- Chicken wings, nobody beats The Moose from back in the day in North Bay. Twenty wings as big as your fist and a pitcher of beer for twenty dollars. Also where I spent my 19th birthday.
- Anything Mexican
- Bulgogi from the Korean restaurant on Rideau Street in Ottawa
- Hummus and babaganoush, Dill di, onions dip, so pretty much any dip, especially the three layer nacho dip made by Grandma and Auntie Alyssa
- Dill pickles and bread and butter pickles
- Crackers and cheese with or without bread and butter pickles

- Pumpkin pie
- Raspberry sour cream pie
- Persians
- Anything with bacon!
- Fry pies from the North Bay farmers market
- Greek food in Ottawa
- Spitz sunflower seeds any kind
- Chips of all kinds, especially ketchup, dill pickle and all dressed
- Doritos all kinds

Japan

Japan's food scene is amazing and always evolving.
I loved many of the things that I ate there and
many things I didn't like. This is the list:

- Sweet and sour pork made in Hidaka Mura, the small town I lived in Japan
- Koroke, which is like a croquette
- Kimchi udon soup
- Any tonkatsu or donkatsu curry, any Japanese curry for that matter
- Edamame
- Tonkatsu
- Donkatsu
- Miso soup
- Gyudon, which is like the Japanese version of bulgogi and consists of sweet seasoned beef mixed up with eggs and rice
- Gyoza, which are dumplings filled with a variety of ingredients. My favourite was pork
- Okonomiyaki a version of a seafood pancake that is delicious
- Karage, which is fried chicken
- Kobe beef
- The best cheeseburger I ever had was in Osaka at
- All Japanese sweet potatoes made any way
- Yuzu juice and the fruit
- Hichews
- Dars chocolate bar

- Sour candy
- Calbee pizza chips
- Tempura anything
- Sushi
- Sashimi, especially katsuo
- Ramen
- Shabu shabu
- Japanese ice cream that you would buy at a convenient store and is a single serving size and comes in all kinds of flavours. My favourite is by Morinaga in a rectangular cone bar of tastiness. The flavours that I would have most often were vanilla and vanilla with solid chocolate layer in the middle
- Yakitori
- Onigiri
- Soba
- Takoyaki
- Twister combo with Gavin at KFC
- Chicken with sun-dried tomatoes from Clare and Gavin
- Matcha
- Japanese energy drinks like Pocari Sweat and Aquarius
- Many types of Japanese beer like Asahi Super Dry, Yebisu, Sapporo, Kirin, and Suntory
- Favorite sakes, Kubota, Hakkaisan, Hakutsuru, and Gekkeikan Junmai
- Favorite Japanese whiskey, Suntory, Hibiki Harmony, Yamazaki, Nikka Coffee Malt and Toki by Suntory
- Shochu

Bahrain

- In my neighborhood of Gufool there was a traditional bakery that did fresh round bread almost like naan bread, and it was delicious. I ate it almost every day for breakfast alternating between plain and cheese-filled. Very similar to khubz
- Hummus with chillies
- Grilled kofta sandwich
- Shawarma
- Black cod fish and chips from the place by JJS Irish Pub

- Sambousa, or samosas
- Halwa
- Baklava
- Curried fish on rice
- Indian food from the local restaurant. I would eat there about once a week and the restaurant owner would take me in the kitchen to show me what they were cooking that day. They made the best onion baji I have ever had. I really enjoyed their butter chicken, briyan and their chana masala
- My favourite place to eat was Monsoon and they had great Thai food, but their ambiance was incredible
- Fresh dates from the date palms
- Efes beer and shisha pipes!
- Fresh juices from the souk
- Fresh spices from the souk
- McArabia meal at McDonald's…Laugh if you want to because it is delicious

Russia

- Borscht by the lady in Sergiev Posad.
- Beef stroganoff
- Street pickles made by little baboushkas. They are sometimes hit and miss, but I had more hits than misses
- Solyanka soup
- Diavola pizza from la Roma in our neighborhood in Moscow. It was the best in town. Great owners who were super friendly
- Olivier, which is Russian potato salad
- Blini which is like a crepe
- Shaslik is a way of barbecuing and it is super-delicious. The best place in Moscow is the Izmaylovo Market. The best place for souvenirs in the city. I went on a regular basis for the pork Shaslik. Totally craving it right now
- Pirozhki kind of like a perogie in a pastry instead
- This is where I invented the Billa Bomber, so see the recipe below
- Best beer in Moscow, Baltika 3, Baltika 7, Bochkarev Svetloe and Stary Melnik

- Best Russian vodka that I had, Putinka, Russian standard, Beluga, Moskovskaya, (Smirnoff and Stolichnaya don't count as not that many Russians drink them)
- Taewon's mom's kimchi and kimchi-jjigae
- This is also where I discovered mama Africa's sauce. Try both the red and green bottles and add them to your stir fry
- Gemma and I also had the most delicious cappuccino cake and we have been searching ever since
- Some great restaurants that we recommend are Il Patio and Planet Sushi, great Italian and Japanese food, especially the Tom kha kai soup
- The Pushkin Café is a must. I took your mom here for our first Valentine's Day and it was amazing
- This is also where I had the second best Shawarma of my life just outside Voykovskaya metro station
- I also had Tibetan cuisine for the first time at Tibetan Gimali with your mom, and I still can't get the soup I had out of my mind. It was called Tibetan soup, I think. I wish I knew what I ate as in the name of the dishes because they were super
- Goodman's Steakhouse is another great place for steak and burgers
- La Cantina is a great place for Mexican food in Moscow and they do really good burritos
- Decent chocolate bars and one of my favourties was Alenka
- Lay's has a big presence here and my favourites were shaslik and mozzarella — super delicious
- Gemma and I went with a group of friends to a Thai restaurant by all the fancy stores and it was the best Thai food that we have had outside of Thailand. Unfortunately, it closed down while we were there.

<u>Singapore</u>

- Ichiban Sushi with the same consistent order: gyoza, edamame (hot), sizzling black pepper beef, potato croquette, vegetable rolls, cucumber rolls, veggie tempura and an Asahi
- Yellow Chairs steak dinner (New Zealand meat), best washed down with a big bottle of ice cold Tiger

- Marina Bay Sands chocolate and cheese buffet
- PS Cafe Wagyu beef burgers or steak sandwiches and any of their desserts, especially the chocolate marshmallow brownies
- Mexcian at Cha Cha Chas, especially the chimichangas
- Baba sheep — chicken cashew
- Brotzeit pork medallions, veal schnitzel
- Chilis burgers were good at Jcube rink
- Hard Rock Cafe on Sentosa great atmosphere and food
- Platinum — movies, popcorn and drinks in style
- Poulet and chicken dish
- Paul's Sandwiches
- Tropical Rainforest Cafe — great Indian food, weird location
- Mandarin Oriental — amazing brunch with free flow champagne, amazing mushroom soup
- Breadtalk — amazing bread roll and doughnuts
- Isetan Bakery for breaky and treats
- Lenas — various different foods, all good
- Subway — veggie sub and tuna sub
- Din Tai Fung — try something different. The dumplings are great
- Turkish/Lebanese restaurant for Shawarma
- Movenpick
- Mezzo Restaurant before watching a shon at Marina Theatres
- French steak restaurant in Clarke Quay, amazing steak. Unfortunately, it has closed down
- Starbucks for caramel cino and sparkling green tea
- Chijmes! Is a cool place to eat
- Brewerkz — great pub food and brewery
- Satay
- Lau Pa Sat — A legendary food court
- Skinny Pizza
- Pandan — cake and bread
- Curry puffs
- Raffles for a Singapore Sling
- Jamie Oliver
- Cure is an awesome restaurant with Andrea and Alan. They took us after I was diagnosed and it completely took our minds of it. The food is amazing there and I highly recommend it

- Wine Connection, which is great for nibbles and drinks
- Italian Osteria for great Italian, especially the pizza bread
- Spruce — an old fire station for their truffle fries
- Singlong black pepper sauce
- Awfully Chocolate
- Stuff D for great wraps
- Japan Street in Jurong Point
- Fat Boys burgers
- The Food Place for pulled pork
- Two for One Canadian Pizza, Sarpinos, Bella Pizzeria — the best I had in Singapore
- Krajnji Farmers Market
- Arab quarter for awesome Middle Eastern food
- Dempsey Hill for great Mexican and the grocers with the playground for kids. Get a good hearty meal here. Everything was good that we ordered
- Blu Kouzina Greek Restaurant for great Greek
- Holland Village has a great array of restaurants and our favourite was Cha Cha Chas
- British Club for many reasons, especially wine tasting nights
- Hainanese chicken rice
- Paris Baguette — crispy chicken salad, tuna sandwich and club sandwich
- Level 33 Microbrewery — a great place for testing different beers
- 12 Cupcakes
- Maya's cooking. She was our helper and looked after Carter full-time. She was fantastic and lovely and kind always.

Thailand

- Krabi Beach Hotel green and red curry as well as pineapple rice watching the sunset
- Cashew chicken at Novotel Karon Beach — best we have ever had in our lives
- Mango sticky rice in Chiang Mai
- Green papaya salad and pad Thai in Chiang Mai
- Yellow Thai curry

- Khao pad, which is fried rice
- Tom yum soup
- Tom ka kai
- Satay with peanut sauce
- Chiang Mai cooking school

Vietnam

- Sweet and sour pork made at the hotel we stayed at was the best we ever had in the world
- Pho
- Spring rolls
- Rau Muong — stir fried morning glory
- Beer that I liked were 333, Bia Hanoi

England

- The full English breakfast
- Eton mess
- Sticky toffee pudding
- Jaxson's BLT
- Any roast dinner by the Lord Poullett in Hinton St. George in Somerset
- Chana masala at Als Tikka in Bristol
- Enid's fish and chips in Bristol
- Any Cadbury chocolate
- Anything Marks and Spencers, especially their green pickled chillies and their Pontefract cakes
- The Gurkha Palace is probably the best Nepalese food outside of Nepal
- Arctic Fox's Glacier Black Licorice Mints
- Chequers have real good food
- The Hangman Pub

USA

- In NY city, the restaurant we had our wedding reception in, Puttanesca, had amazing pizza and our wedding menu was as follows:
- Planet Hollywood
- The hole in the wall burger place in the fancy hotel that Nadine and Rossy showed us
- A pub right by Nadine's sister's husband liquor store
- Old Homestead Steakhouse — amazing burger share with Uncle Gary on New Year's Eve
- The Venetian Hotel Vegas had great steak
- Rat Pack Restaurant — not sure of the name but it had great pasta and pizza
- Japanese restaurant at the Mirage Hotel before seeing *The Love*
- Castle Hotel — good breakfast with a show
- At the ranch in the Grand Canyon — a great chilli after the helicopter ride

Jamaica

- Jerk chicken
- Jerk pork
- Jerk goat
- Jamaican patties
- Red Stripe beer
- Dirty banana cocktail
- Plantains
- Appleton rum

Cuba

- Ropa vieja
- Cubano
- Moros y Cristianos
- Roast pork
- plantains
- Dulce de mango

- Dulce de guava
- Plantain chips
- Cristal beer and Bucanero beer
- Cuban rum any kind
- Mojitos
- Cuba Libre with Tukola
- Daiquiri at the Dupont Mansion

France

- Any café with an outdoor patio for pastries and people watching
- Japanese restaurant in the Montparnasse area. It was pouring rain and we decided to go see *Avatar*. We have never seen a movie theatre so busy before. It was insane

Cambodia

- Pub street in Siem Reap — lots of cool places to eat and some crazy street food if you dare
- There is a great place in Siem Reap that does steak sandwiches
- Indian place across from our hotel in Phnom Phen

Malaysia

- Hard Rock Cafe in Melaka
- Tallest peak in Langkawi at the bottom had cool shops and a great restaurant
- Sunset cruise from Langkawi with a BBQ chicken Satay
- Eastern Oriental Hotel in Penang — amazing breakfast buffet and restaurants to eat, good place for a Sunday roast but we missed that unfortunately

Kuwait

- Dates in the desert with camel farmers
- Traditional bread and hummus in the souk
- Eating at the sheik's house, especially the Shawarma and smoking of the shisha pipes

Australia

- Fish and chips in Rosebud outside of Melbourne
- Cute side streets in Melbourne, some great pasta
- Check out the pubs downtown in Sydney, there are some great pizzas with lots of interesting toppings
- The oldest pub in Sydney — there is an awesome pizzeria very close that is always busy
- Manley Island — take a boat from Sydney Harbour. A good burger and homemade chips with a selection of different beers at the microbrewery
- Greek restaurant in Cairns, brilliant food
- The hotel we stayed at in Cairns had some really amazing food and some pre-dinner snacks as well
- Jus Burgers
- Jamie Oliver's in Perth
- By the train station and Jamie Oliver's was a great place for ribs. We are unsure of the name
- Margaret River chocolate and nougat place full of delicious treats
- Monkey Brewery for beers
- The pub in Margaret River town that has a smoker smelt great. We just missed the night it happened, but they had great food
- The little chapel for a good BLT

New Zealand

- Great steak and ale pie at a pub right by the marina
- A good place to eat in Rotorua is the place with a bunch of restaurants
- The Christmas dinner at the Wellington Hotel
- Steak and ale pie at a pub right by our hotel in Wellington. It was the first time that Carter tried a steak and ale pie. He loved it
- Sky Tower Hotel across from the Sky Tower. It had an amazing bar with free appetizers for guests and they were really fantastic. The restaurant had really great pizza as well
- Hokey Pokey anything

- Black licorice
- The Green Dragon Inn, Hobbiton. Great beef and ale pie. Super beer and the best I had in New Zealand. Maybe it tasted so great because I had just finished carrying Carter for the past two hours. The tour is pretty amazing and beautiful scenery. I highly recommend it. This is also another time when I saved the day for your mom

<u>Ireland - Dublin</u>

- Irish stew in a few pubs that we ate in was amazing and portions were giant
- You have to go to the Guinness Brewery — it is the best brewery tour we have ever been on
- There is a restaurant where you can watch traditional Irish dancing and you can pour your own beer

<u>Scotland</u>

- We mostly ate at our host's house and never out of Logie Coldstone except for the night of the Kaylee in the village hall
- On the Dean sibling trip we had some good eats in Edinburgh, especially at the pub across the street from Edinburgh Dungeon
- Dean's shortbread cookies

<u>Wales</u>

- Full disclosure: I have not had a lot to eat in Wales, but I did have chips and curry sauce on the island of Barry made famous by Gavin and Stacey, and it was tasty.

<u>Czech Republic</u>

The best pizza I have ever had in my life was here. I don't know how to explain it other than dumb luck. I was visiting Prague to get my hockey fix while the NHL was on strike. I went with a guy I worked with who I called "Grandpa" since he looked like he could be one. It was really chucking it down in Prague so since we didn't want to be out in the freezing rain, we decided to go and see *Ocean's 12* at the nearby shopping mall. We had time to eat before the movie and we came across a pizzeria that had a wood fired oven. How good was it? We went back two more times before we left. That is where I fell in love with the diavola pizza

- goulash that we ate at an underground restaurant
- Apple strudel in Prague Castle
- Assorted cuts of meat, most importantly sausage
- Best beer Pilsner Urquell, Kozel, Staropramen, Krusovice
- Absinthe

Norway

- I didn't have too many traditional foods while I was in Oslo, but whatever I ate was delicious
- Apple strudel just outside of Oslo
- Widest array of black licorice candies I have ever seen
- Ringnes beer

Bali

- Cafe Lotus — sit and relax by the lotus flowers enjoying a club sandwich and spring rolls
- Cafe Luna — good drinks and cakes plus some live music in the evening
- Miro's Restaurant — amazing food with brilliant seating, huge portions and super cheap
- OOPP's coconut curry served in a coconut — delicious plus buy one get one free drinks in the evening. Make sure you dump your rice into your curry
- Gelato next to OOPP's was the best ever, plus dairy free! Had one nearly every night
- The Mansion Hotel where we stayed had a lovely dinner and an amazing breakfast every day
- Elephant Safari Park had great food plus you could hang out with the elephants

- After white water rafting we tucked into a traditional Balinese lunch
- We did a bike ride that started with lunch overlooking a volcano. Amazing views

Bintan and Batam

- Nirwana Hotel — usually a carb dinner as Gemma would be usually racing here
- The hotel we stayed at in Batam and the one next to us both had good food and breakfast. Shame the window fell out of the room when we opened it!

Italy - Venice

- The Hard Rock Cafe for the appetizer platter was tasty and we had the benefit of snow falling outside, and it was beautiful
- Great pasta and pizza everywhere. No great meals but no bad ones. The city is an excellent place for just walking around and of course gondola rides. It is such a beautiful city, so you can understand why I proposed to Gemma here

Netherlands

- Café just outside of the train station downtown

UAE, Dubai and Abu Dhabi

- Brunch at aunty Amy's club
- Frozen yogurt
- Five Guy's burgers at the Dubai mall
- The dates from the souk stuffed with almonds covered in chocolate and coconut
- Any chocolate-covered dates and camel milk chocolate
- The Ritz-Carlton Abu Dhabi for lunch

Philippines - Boracay

- TGIF for decent food but spectacular sunset
- The hotel restaurant on the beach
- Dried mango
- The barbecue restaurant by the shopping centre
- The Greek restaurant by the barbecue restaurant

Hong Kong

- Street beer under bamboo scaffolding with Shawn drinking Tsing Tao
- Wraps that we ate with Tex were amongst the best we ever had
- Lots of great restaurants in HK like the Korean restaurant up the escalators not far from our hotel
- Great Italian place that Gemma and I went to with Tex
- Marks and Spencers for quick and easy food when you are out and about
- Ice cream at the top of the peak
- We ate in a rough Japanese restaurant just off the market but it was not bad considering the look and condition of the restaurant. It was super busy, which means delicious or cheap… this place was in the middle

Macau

- Portuguese chicken

Taiwan

- Din Tai Fung at Taipei 101 for delicious dumplings
- Shilin Night Market for pork buns and Taiwan beer and peanut brittle and pineapple cakes
- There is a decent Mexican restaurant in Taipei
- Pizza from the back of a pickup truck that had a brick pizza oven in Kao Shiung during Gemma's first Ironman race

- In Taipei close to Taipei 101 is a shopping mall and at the top was an Italian restaurant and I had an amazing pizza that I would rank top five in the world

For breakfast

French Toast

Crack an egg into a bowl and add one cup of milk, a teaspoon of cinnamon and a tablespoon of vanilla. Then whisk the bowl until everything is blended together. Turn on the stove to medium and place the frying pan on the stove. Dip both sides of the bread in the bowl and then put it in the frying pan until they are golden brown. Enjoy with maple syrup.

For lunch and dinner

Kimchi Soup Inspired by Gavin

Find a kimchi that you love. Use either chicken, beef or vegetable stock as your base. Choose the vegetables that you want to go with the soup, chop them up and put them in the pot. Add the amount of water that your base requires. Then bring to a boil while stirring. Then add the kimchi and cook for five minutes. Throw in udon noodles. While it cools, add pepper to taste and eat with chopsticks. Carter, you ate this before and loved it. For extra spice you can add Indian green pickled chillies (Pataks or mother's recipe).

Indian Grilled Cheese

This is made the same way as any grilled cheese but adding green pickled chillies on top of the cheese before cooking (Pataks or mother's recipe) and dipping in ketchup.

Chili

This is best done in a slow cooker. You will need: two cans of Heinz beans, one can of kidney beans, one can of black beans, one can of diced tomatoes, one can of stewed tomatoes, frozen vegetables of your choice, around a pound of beef, a jar of spaghetti sauce of your choice and a packet of President's Choice chili powder. Mix all of the ingredients and cook on low while you are at work. If you want to be brave you could try making a chilasgna or a chili shepherd's pie or even mix your chili with rice and make chili cabbage rolls. Even a chili pie instead of a meat pie.

Japanese Curry

This is easy to do. Buy any Japanese curry and follow the instructions on the box. Choose your meat and vegetables that you want. Stir fry your meat and vegetables first and then mix them together with the curry. Choose either the Uncle Ben's wild rice or garden rice to eat it with, or change the rice for udon noodles.

Puff Pastry Chicken

Get some puff pastry and cut it into squares. Take your chicken and cut it into small pieces to fit your squares. Add cheese and broccoli. Then follow the instructions on how to bake the puff pastry. You can use any type of marinade for your meat and vegetables that you like.

Egg Rolls

You need a green cabbage, egg roll wrappers, bean sprouts and chicken (can put whatever you want really), soy sauce, and salt and pepper, a pinch of sugar. Cut everything into thin strips. Stir fry the cabbage first then add soy sauce and sugar. Stir fry the chicken separately adding salt and pepper to taste. Then mix it all together with the bean sprouts. And stir fry together until the bean sprouts look wilted slightly. Then drain any extra liquid. Get your egg roll wrappers and place some of your stir fry in the middle of the wrapper. Use egg as a glue and crimp them shut with a fork. Finally deep fry until golden brown. Enjoy.

Koroke

You need panko crumbs, one egg, ground beef, onions, potatoes, salt and pepper. Stir fry your beef and onions with some salt and pepper.

Boil the potatoes and then mix them together with the beef and onions. Then follow the instructions for the panko crumbs. Deep fry in oil until golden brown. Enjoy with bulldog tonkatsu sauce or any kind of sauce that you want.

Singlong Black pepper beef

Stir fry your choice of vegetables and cabbage, purple and green. Then add your beef with the sauce. It is a bit spicy but delicious. Serve with rice.

Drinks I Invented

Indian Caesar

Prepare your glass as you would normally. Two fingers of Russian standard and a tablespoon-teaspoon of green pickled chillies (Pataks or mother's recipe), smush them up and fill your glass with clamato juice. Garnish with a piece of celery and a dill carrot or pickle. Also tastes great without the vodka.

Billa Bomber

This drink is best for a hot day. You need blood orange juice, a berry fruit yogurt drink/smoothie (Nestlé or Yoplait) and vodka. Two fingers of Russian standard, one third cup of yogurt drink and the rest blood orange juice.

Dessert

Butterscotch Chipits Cookies — from Hershey.com slightly modified

INGREDIENTS

3/4 cup butter or margarine, softened (175 mL)
3/4 cup granulated sugar (175 mL)
3/4 cup packed light brown sugar (175 mL)
2 eggs (2)

1 tbsp vanilla extract (15 mL)
1-1/4 cups all-purpose flour (300 mL)
1 tsp baking soda (5 mL)
1 tsp ground cinnamon (5 mL)
1/2 tsp salt (2 mL)
3 cups dry quick-cooking or regular rolled oats (750 mL)
1-3/4 cups CHIPITS Butterscotch Chips (425 mL)

DIRECTIONS

1. Preheat oven to 375°F (190°C).
2. Beat butter with granulated sugar and brown sugar in a large bowl until well blended. Add eggs and vanilla; beat well.
3. Combine flour with baking soda, cinnamon and salt; gradually add to butter mixture, beating until well combined. Stir in oats and butterscotch chips; mix well. Drop by heaping teaspoons onto ungreased baking sheets.
4. Bake for 8 to 10 minutes or until golden brown. Cool slightly; transfer to a rack and cool completely.

Makes about 4 dozen cookies.

<u>Cheesecake from Kraft — some modifications</u>

What You Need

1-1/2 cups graham cracker crumbs
3 Tbsp. sugar
1/3 cup butter or margarine, melted
4 pkg. (8 oz. each) PHILADELPHIA Cream Cheese, softened
1 cup sugar
1 tbsp. vanilla
4 eggs

Smucker's Caramel Sauce and Pecans

Let's Make It

1. Heat oven to 325°F.
2. Combine graham crumbs, 3 Tbsp. sugar and butter; press onto bottom of 9-inch springform pan.
3. Beat cream cheese, 1 cup sugar and vanilla with mixer until blended. Add eggs, 1 at a time, mixing on low speed after each just until blended. Pour over crust.
4. Bake 55 min. or until centre is almost set. Run knife around rim of pan to loosen cake; cool before removing rim. Refrigerate cheesecake 4 hours.
5. Cover cheesecake in pecans and then caramel sauce. Or any topping of your choosing.

Pumpkin Dip — Jill's recipe with my modification

Two bricks of cream cheese
Two cups of icing sugar
One can of pumpkin pie mix
One tablespoon of vanilla extract

Mix all of the ingredients with a hand blender and chill. Serve with ginger snaps.

Chapter Thirty

Important Messages I Gave

The Matt Barker Exchange

First day back from Japan here and I just downloaded and listened to the song. Matt, that's some beautiful stuff. I'm left without words, and am so grateful — not just for the song, but all that it represents. Our shared childhood, our friendship.

Who was playing and singing?

I should confess that I recorded songs for you too, a few months back. Well, they were for your whole family really, perhaps mostly your two boys. But then I opted against sharing them (and others I intended to record), thinking they would just be too sad to bear. The backstory will help explain.

After that early March day when you told me of your diagnosis, it occupied my mind much of the time. One of the times it stuck in mind most was when I was putting Thomas (our three-year-old) to bed at nights, as I thought about how you must be feeling when putting Carter (and a couple of months later, Harrison) to bed. I usually sing a few songs to Thomas. One night while starting that routine and thinking about you, *Helpless* came to mind and so I sang it to Thomas. ("There is a town in North Ontario...") He loved it instantly and within a couple of days was singing along at bedtime. I came to love those bed times because they were a mix of joy and sorrow. Sorry because you really are in a "helpless" situation, but also joy in a young child singing through the words at the same time.

Somehow the sorrow came to feel therapeutic in a way — as though it were better to struggle through it in a song, than to ignore it. Then I thought you might feel similarly about that song playing at bedtime, so I played and recorded a version of it. A very slow version. That got me thinking I should record a few more songs, a bedtime EP, which your kids might still enjoy after you're gone. I was thinking about five songs would be good, so there was the task of choosing four more. To help pick, I decided on two criteria. Each song should conjure that therapeutic mix of joy and sorrow that *Helpless* did, and each should also have some Canadian connection.

So the next song I recorded was an acoustic version of *Good Times*, a Tom Cochrane song.

But then as I listened several times to the two songs I had recorded thus far, it started to seem like a bad idea to share them. I feared they'd just invoke too much sadness for you, in the near term anyway.

I'm still inclined to think that way. The last thing I want to do is make your pain even worse. Even just telling you this story runs that risk. But it now seems right to share at least the story, now that you've shared *Sugar Mountain*. The song you shared is something I'll always treasure, and which will always return me vividly to our youthful days.

So now that that's all said, are you feeling any better from the stem cell treatment? Has it helped at all?

Matt

--

Hey Matt, well, you convinced me I should share the two songs I've recorded thus far for your Bedtime EP. I'm not sure when I'll get to add other songs — my recording space in the basement is in upheaval after the home renos.

The two songs that are here are not fully finished. I asked Matt Boyer to lay down a track with a weird new instrument (Seaboard) he's got, and he did record that track and send it to me; I still plan to add that into *Helpless* sometime. But the two files here are semi-finished now.

I hope these don't bring too much sadness, as I had feared before. My initial hope was, as I tried to say in more detail in the previous email, that the sadness would be therapeutic in a way. I sure hope that's true.

I also hope your family is doing as well as they can. It looks from Facebook like your two boys are getting in some good summer cottage time — great stuff.

Matt

--

Me:

It is always hard to face your inevitable death. No matter what I do, I cry every day about what I will miss. I won't be there for Gemma, my kids, my family or my friends. It is torture of my soul to the highest degree and it is a relentless constant. I have treasured our friendship since we were children and all of the great times we had. Many of my fondest memories include you and your family. How many Barkerovs are there? You are the only ones that I know and I lived in Mother Russia so I know best. I want to thank you for your songs and everything that we have shared over my lifetime. I love you like a brother and I always have. I will share the songs with my family so they can understand how much you have impacted me.

--

Matt

Brother, those words were at once some of the most warming and hardest I've ever read. I wish so much that I could help you, but I know

I'm helpless. I can't imagine what you're going through, though I know that you struggle most with thinking about your family and friends. When I had the stroke last year and things were iffy for a short time, it wasn't me that I was worried about, but instead those I would leave behind if it went badly. And I know that this is exactly what is torturing you, and to a far greater degree that I can't even pretend to comprehend. All I can say is that you have my undying support, my deepest sadness, and the lasting fact that we shared a wonderful childhood together — that is something I shall always cherish. Love is one of those rare, pure, shining things that death never, ever, touches.

Matt

--

Gavin and Clare on Their Wedding Day

Dear Gavin and Clare,

The modest definition of the word friend is: A person whom one knows, likes, and trusts. One who supports, sympathizes with, and most importantly is understanding.

Love is defined as: A deep, tender, ineffable feeling of affection and solicitude toward a person, recognition of attractive qualities, or a sense of underlying oneness.

Since you are here for this joyous occasion, you know you are looking at those definitions standing before you. It is unfortunate that I cannot be there today to celebrate in your happiness. I have found it a privilege to know you the last three years, and most importantly to be your friend.

When I first met Gavin, it was in Kochi, a delightful city in sunny southern Japan. Surprisingly enough, Clare was not there. Clare was to join Gavin in the weeks to come for an adventure of a lifetime.

Personally, it took a fraction of a second to understand after meeting Clare that Gavin and Clare make a sensational match. As cliché as that sounds, it is something that just makes sense. It shines through in the way they talk to each other, the way they support each other, the way they love their family and friends. It is love in its truest form. It is one that is guided by destiny, for spending one minute with either one of them and you realise that they are genuine. They offer sound advice for those intimate moments, and will provide the hug when you are in need of it most. And most importantly it is done unconditionally.

I was fortunate enough to spend Christmas in Bristol last year, and after meeting some of their family members it furthered my belief that this is an outstanding partnership in love. As I have spent a lot of quality time over the last three years with Gavin and Clare, it is my hope that we will always be in each other's lives. To share in all of the joys that are to be had, and all of the trials and tribulations that accompany the joys.

They say that the most important people you meet and create friendships with are those from your younger days of high school or university. I want to clarify that, perhaps redefine it, to include Japan.

I love you both and I look forward to seeing you in Canada during your honeymoon.

Love Matt

PS: Boobies

I wrote that letter before you got married in 2005. We have had many adventures since then and an incalculable amount of laughs. The fact that my last holiday with Gemma and Carter with Harrison on board was a fitting end. Our trip to New Zealand will always shine brilliantly even though the depressing news was looming on the horizon in a way that I seemed to be the only one that could see it.

Our walk on the beach was the first time that I really cried. It was a sobbing wail that was embarrassing, but Gavin thank you for holding on to me and comforting me in the preamble for what was to come in the new year. I never really thanked you for that. But I know that it wasn't necessary because it never was. Our friendship, and I include you Clare as well when I say this, was never based on anything but love. Love for good times, good music, good food, laughter and most importantly, love for each other. Knowing the two of you for this long has been a really great ride and I don't want to get off, but ALS is causing our ride to come to a horrific life-changing derailment where I won't be able to serenade you with my ridiculous songs about boobies!

Thank you Kelly

Hi Kelly,

It has been eighteen years since I last saw you and you look the same. It was really kind of you to make that message for me. It brought a smile to my face and warmed my heart. I am so fortunate to have people in my life like Don who has always been a great friend to me. It will be a wonderful keepsake for my children so that they can know more about their dad. I want to thank you for all of the things that you said, but without people like you giving your time, none of those moments would have been possible. Especially my goal, was it the five hole? Thanks again for everything.

Your friend,

Monte

My Love of Music and a Special Thank You to the Downies and The Tragically Hip

Dear everyone,

I have loved learning how to play music, and I don't think that I would have loved it as much without Gord and the Tragically Hip. I really don't. You inspired me to learn the guitar and write my own songs. You also inspired me to do a mini farewell tour of my own to say goodbye to people who were special to me. Your music was the soundtrack to the majority of my life with other bands and artists filling in the rest. You have been with me during all of the trials and tribulations of my youth where in the affairs of the heart we are all fifteen.

My all-time favourite album is *Phantom Power* and it is the first album that I learned to play a whole song. Membership was taught to me by my good friend, Davis, aka Hamlet, during the most important and amazing summer of my life. I was working for the Tim Horton's Children's Foundation in Kananaskis, Alberta, and that album was the album of the summer. Whenever I would hear or play one of *Phantom Power*'s songs it would transport me right back to that glorious summer. It was a major turning point in my life and where I decided that I would become a teacher.

I saw this tour in Sudbury where I went to school with Andrew Fuller who would tell me great things about the Hip and how he knew them because he was basically babysat by them. Only in Canada would something like this happen.

All of your music is linked to the happiest memories of my life and unfortunately some of the saddest ones. However, it always soothed my soul and the hard times became a softer shade of grey. For example, I want you to know that when I was in the hospital for the final round of testing before my diagnosis, I had trouble sleeping. So I put *A World Possessed By The Human Mind* on repeat and it reduced my anxiety to the point of sleep and a restful one. Well as restful as could be for someone that knew inside that they were dying. I often wondered what Gord was feeling when he decided to keep working. For me, it was panic that spurred me to do this, to leave my children something so they know about me and how much I love them. I want to thank you for helping me realise what I needed to do with my final days. I have attached a photo of a painting that my friend made for me when she heard that I was diagnosed with ALS. I feel like it is a good representation of who we are as Canadians, and we have all of you to thank for that.

Sincerely,

Matt Dean

Dear Ellen

Dear Ellen,

My name is Matt Dean and I am dying. I was diagnosed with ALS on February 28 of this year. My family's world was turned upside down and blown to smithereens. I don't know how much time I have left since my form of ALS is progressing rapidly. I have already lost the ability to look after myself in a few short months. I would like to do something special for my wife, Gemma. She is my wife of a lifetime. I couldn't have been luckier if I tried. You name it, she does it. There are no words to convey or express my love for her.

I met Gemma in Moscow ten years ago, and we have been together ever since. Knowing that you are dying is never easy, especially when you are leaving the love of your life behind with our two boys (Carter is twenty-two months old and Harrison is five months old.). She is the most beautiful person I have ever known. This disease is taking everything from me, and I want to do something special for her.

So what can I do to show her how much I love and adore her? How can I show her how much I appreciate everything she has done for me but most importantly our boys? Could you please help me to do something for her? Gemma's dream has always been to race at Kona in the Ironman. Is this possible?

Sincerely,

Matt Dean

To My Nonie and Pop Pops

I guess I want to tell you that I love you, and I wish that you would have taken the dirt nap first. I was planning on doing your eulogy but ALS has ruined that. I was incredibly honored to give Pop Pops' eulogy and I wanted to make you proud. That is all I ever wanted. So what can I do? Here is the song that I wrote for you a few years ago.

Nonie's Wooden Spoon Song

Holy moly, me oh my,
She's got that look in her eye,
She's gone to the kitchen drawer,

Ha ha Matt she's gonna smack,
That big grin right off your chin,
And I'm gonna laugh at you,

She'll hit me with the wooden spoon,
Break it on my butt in two,
All while saying I love you,

Oh well, what can I say,
It is your big birthday,
Not everyone's as old as dirt,

Not everyone makes 91,
And if you hit me on the bum,
You won't make 92,

Oh yeah, it's OK,
I lived to see another day,
And I still love you,

So I'll come home,
I'll come home,
I'll come home to see you,

And if you hit me,
With a wooden spoon,
You won't see 92,

So I'll come home,
I'll come home,
I'll come cuz I love you.

Thank you for being the best grandma and grandpa that we could ever have hoped for. And for teaching us the meaning of family. I will love you always.

Made in the USA
Monee, IL
30 September 2020

43630847R00118